SELF COACHING 101

Use Your Mind—
Don't Let It Use You!

By

Brooke Castillo

www.brookecastillo.com
Email: brooke@coach4weight.com

ISBN: 978-0-9778539-9-1

Cover design: Cathi Stevenson

Page design: Janice Phelps Williams
www.janicephelps.com

PRINTED IN THE UNITED STATES OF AMERICA

For Chris.

Every girl should be so lucky.

Acknowledgments

Read this! It matters to me that you read this. I want you to know about all the amazing people who made this book happen, even though their names do not appear on the cover. These are my peeps. I love these folks. I want you to know about them.

I have to give a big shout out to **my publishing team.** God knows I could not have written a book that could be sold for a dime without them. Janice Phelps— who makes the inside look pretty and fresh—you are a gem with tremendous patience. To Allison at Booksurge who has done this (twice!) with me—you are a saint. Thanks to proofreaders Anna Paradox and First Editing who made the text readable. Huge big thanks to Cathi Stevenson, who designed the cover. You are a little bit of heaven wrapped up in a designer who gets it right on the first try. Thank you so much for putting up with me.

I have to give big huge hugs of love to **my family**, especially to my husband, Chris, who is the most amazing man I have ever met. He once told me, "The planet is a better place because you are in it," as if it were an irrefutable fact. I love this man! To my kids, Christian and Connor for being excited about everything—including mom's name on the cover of a book. "Oh my gosh, Mom, look! It says Brooke Castillo on this book!"

To Liz Jarrett for always being in a good mood, for being so easy to be with, for her killer sense of humor, amazing laugh and for loving my brother. To Aaron and Matt for reminding me that no matter how much fan mail I get, I am still very easy to make fun of. To Wendy for always responding, "Of course," whenever I inform her of a new accomplishment. I am blessed to have her as my sister. To my mom and Dennis for making us all family. Love isn't big enough a word.

And of course I have to thank **my girls.** To Erika for her unconditional love and for keeping all my teenage secrets—I love her so big! To Suyin for being, hands down, my biggest fan. She knows all my faults and still applauds me any chance she gets. My eyes fill with tears when I think about how deeply I love and adore her. To Jo for all the laughs and for loving life without the rules as much as I do. To Marik for listening to anything no matter what or when—I cherish her friendship deeply. To Meadow for mocking me when I start to feel sorry for myself—I love this girl (twice). And to Martha for being brilliant, hilarious, crazy and loving—I have to thank her for insisting I write this book.

And finally, a big Thank You **to You** for reading my stuff, hiring me to coach you, listening to my audios and letting me know you enjoy it. You (yeah you) really matter to me.

Table of Contents

Permissions

Please reprint, publish and share any part of this book with anyone who you think might benefit from it. I just ask that you please include the following with any portion you reprint: Reprinted with Permission from the Author Brooke Castillo (www.brookecastillo.com)

"If you have the same damn thoughts,
you're gonna have the same damn day."

–Meadow DeVor

Foreword

WHO THE HECK IS BROOKE CASTILLO?

When I was younger I was taught how to walk, how to eat, how to read, how to add, and even how to drive a car. No one ever taught me how to think. They taught me what to think and why I should think what they told me, but they never taught me how to think a thought purposefully. I never took a class in thought management, in fact, I didn't even know that managing my thoughts was an option.

Later, when I went to college and studied Psychology, I learned that we do have some ability to manage our thoughts but this was only really necessary if we were suffering from some abnormal psychiatric condition that made us non-functional in the world. In other words, everything they taught me was so that I could help my patients within the medical model—not so I could help myself.

I went through life, like many of my clients, thinking what I was told to think or shown by example what and how to think. I believed the recycled thoughts of my parents and their parents. My young mind's programming went unquestioned and remained mainly out of my conscious awareness through many years of suffering and negative emotion. My negative thoughts ultimately led to negative results that seemed out of my control.

Now I know better.

Now I know that every thought we think can be a choice we make. I know now that I can retrain my mind to think in ways that bring me positive emotion and therefore positive results. I realize that it is not just what I happen to think in any moment that will determine the outcome of my life, but what I WANT to think that will bring me everything I desire and more.

I often say to my clients that someone should pull us aside at about age 25 and let us know that we can now stop borrowing our parents' thought patterns. They could fill us in on the truth that true adulthood is emotional adulthood which requires that we think for ourselves.

That someone for me came in the form of multiple authors. They have taught me and shown me how to become an emotionally mature adult by managing my own thinking and coaching myself into a much more abundant and positive life. I will refer to them throughout the book by first name. This is not a sign of disrespect, but rather one of familiarity and deep love for each of them.

My Favorite Teachers are:

Eckhart Tolle: Author of *The Power of Now*, *A New Earth*, and many more. He can be found at www.eckharttolle.com. I call him Eckhart in this book. Oprah calls him a prophet.

Byron Katie: Author of *Loving What Is* and *I Need Your Love—Is That True?* She can be found at www.thework.com. I call her Katie in this book. We call her work as important as breathing.

Abraham: Author of *Ask and it is Given, The Law of Attraction, The Amazing Power of Deliberate Intent, The Astonishing Power of Emotions,* and *Money and the Law of Attraction.* Abraham, along with Jerry and Esther Hicks, have the most thorough teachings of the Law of Attraction on the market through their books, tapes and videos. I have learned so much from reading and listening to their work. I refer to them, and their collective work, as Abraham in this book. Their website is www.abraham-hicks.com.

Jill Bolte Taylor: Author of *A Stroke of Insight.* She is a Harvard trained PhD who studies the brain and knows words like neurosymmetry. She is super smart and I should probably call her Dr. Taylor, but it feels too formal. She is so loving I want to give her a hug and call her Jill. I hope she doesn't mind. I am sure her right brain won't. You can find her on the web at www.speakers.ca/bolte-taylor_jill.aspx.

Martha Beck: Author of *The Joy Diet, Finding Your Own North Star* and many more. She is another Harvard PhD, who is scary smart; but her sick sense of humor and love of gel pens makes it impossible to call her doctor (not to mention she won't allow it). I lovingly refer to her as "Martha" in this book. Find more about her at www.MarthaBeck.com.

Tony Robbins: I know. I know. I almost didn't include him because it is a little embarrassing to admit he is one of my most influential teachers. But there is really no denying it. If you have read *Awaken the Giant Within,* you know what I mean. Yes, the guy has big teeth and talks with a bit too much enthusiasm—but he is frickin' brilliant when it comes down to it. He has made a billion dollars in self-help. He may be salesy—but you don't make that kind of money and have his kind of staying power without substance to your work. Some of his tools are so kick-butt we have to give Tony his due. I refer to him as "Tony" in this book. You can find more about him at www.tonyrobbins.com.

Pema Chodron: I love Pema! She is a Buddhist Nun in Maine who teaches meditation and writes books. She is brilliant and funny and serene and uses the word "bullshit" on one of her meditation tapes. That was the moment I fell for her—my kind of nun. She has written many awesome books and you can find out more about her at www.shambhala.org/teachers/pema/.

This is by no means a complete list. I have read many, many more books by other brilliant teachers, but if I could wave my magic wand, this is the group I would have out to dinner at Chili's ("Table for eight please.") to talk about life and how our thinking determines so much of its outcome.

My teachers, I have noticed, are all pretty much saying the same things. At times, when I read their works, I wonder if they all know each other and talk to each other before they write. They use different words to talk about similar things.

For example, here is what each of them says on thought:

Katie: "There is always a particular thought that triggers any stressful feeling."

Eckhart: "Unconscious thought alone is the cause of emotional pain."

Jill: "There has been nothing more empowering than the realization that I don't have to think thoughts that bring me pain."

Abraham: "When you think a thought that is not in vibrational alignment with your overall intent, your Inner Being will offer you a negative emotion."

Martha: "All human suffering comes from your thoughts."

Tony: "Holding a limiting thought is the same as systemically ingesting small doses of arsenic... we don't die immediately; we start dying emotionally the moment we partake of them."

Pema: "It isn't the things that happen to us in our lives that cause us to suffer, it's how we relate to the things that happen to us that causes us to suffer."

I believe each of the authors and teachers above wrote from a place of individual thought, and yet they were so tuned into the truth of the universe that they tapped it as a common brilliance. Do we all have the same access to this brilliance? I believe we do, but maybe not in the exact same ways. Katie and Eckhart both woke up one morning enlightened and never looked back. Abraham is a non-physical channeled entity. Martha has the IQ of a genius, Jill had a left hemisphere stroke, and Tony has a brain tumor that I am convinced pushes on the brilliant part of his brain.

No such luck for me.

And I am guessing not for you either.

I am not enlightened nor a genius. I have had no brain abnormalities that help me detach from negative thinking. I am just like you. I am a mother of two who has to get my kids to school, their homework done, and their lunches made. I write, coach, grocery shop, read, work-out, and pay my bills. I have two very needy dogs. I am not always in the present moment. I don't meditate for hours or enter Nirvana when I do the dishes. I can't sit on a park bench and revel in the magnificence of the universe without hallucinogenic assistance. I don't channel non-physical entities and I have never gotten a call-from Oprah Winfrey. I drink Diet Coke, color my hair, and spend an outrageous amount of money on handbags and my car. I yell at my kids sometimes, whine to my husband, argue with my mother, and I read *People* magazine. Need I say more?

I am a student. I benefit from these teachers and their intelligence. I find my own small piece of enlightenment, Nirvana, and genius in moments of my life through study and application of these universal principles.

My value-add is that I can give it to you quickly. I can give you what I believe are the common truths of each of these amazing teachers. I can apply the truths they share, and retell them in easy-to-understand language to get it into your life fast. I always say to my accountant, "Please explain this to me like I am a third grader." That is what I am good at doing with self-help concepts. I am good at telling you the common truths in my own simplified language.

Here are my notes from what I have learned in my most recent round of self-help study and application. The ideas are not original, but the way I have packaged them is original and straight from my own brain. This information has not been presented quite this way before—as far as I know. It has been life changing for me to apply this one tool to my life and it has worked for thousands of my students and clients.

I first offered this material as a free class on my website: www.selfcoaching101.com, which has had thousands of students. It is still available for download on my site, www.brookecastillo.com. This book will also be available in audio form on my site and on Amazon.com.

Why Use this Model?

"Because it can change your life permanently."

So, you ask, why should I read this book and use Brooke Castillo's model?

Because it works. Period. If you use this model, you will become aware of your thoughts. You will become more conscious. You will become more awakened. You will discover the cause behind your negative emotions. You will have a way to feel better.

In short, it looks like this: It doesn't matter what terms you use, but the part of you that thinks (your ego, your left brain) is the part of you that brings you suffering. Jill says it is a small peanut-sized part of your brain (a collection of cells) that tells stories about what is happening to you in your life. The bummer about this little peanut of neurology is that it is not always a happy storyteller. Many times, Peanut spins a tale of woe. Many times, Peanut lies and tells us horrible, untrue stories. Stories like, "Your Thighs are Too Big," "Everybody is Out to Get You," "You Missed Your

Chance at Success," and "Your Husband Should Behave Differently." This chatter box, Peanut, creates so much suffering that many of us spend our entire lives caught in Peanut Story Hell. The biggest bummer is that most of us don't even realize it is going on!

No one ever took us aside in high school and said, "Hey, you know that voice inside your head that tells you that you are ugly and not popular? That's not you." My best friend in high school asked me if I wanted to get high—not if I wanted to align with my Consciousness and become aware of the thoughts that create my reality. And so I went through most of my adult life living out the unconscious thoughts of my Peanut. My guess is that you have too. My guess is that many of you still are.

Even if Eckhart had pulled me out of class my senior year and suggested I live a life of Awakened Action, I know I wouldn't have listened. I hardly listened when Tony said I could make a million dollars if I monitored my thoughts. It seemed so much easier to just drown them out with alcohol, drugs, sex, and food.

My thoughts were painful—but I didn't know this. I thought it was my life that was painful. I didn't see that I needed to change the thoughts in my mind—I thought I needed to change my life. But as you will see from the model you learn in this book, if you change your actions and results without changing their cause, you are setting yourself up for a cycle of misery. This is why I kept losing weight and gaining it back. I never figured out why I was gaining it in the first place.

It is like those lottery winners who lose all their money. They changed their result—but the thoughts that were keeping them poor were more powerful. Truly, changing our thoughts is the only thing I have found that works to change our results.

This is why the Law of Attraction is so hot right now. It is the truth. Thinking. Thoughts. Mind. Brain. Neuroscience. Cognition. Ego. Pain-Body. Beliefs. Focus. Call it whatever the heck you want—the bottom line is this:

When you think a thought—you feel a feeling. When you feel a feeling—you take action or not because of how you feel. Your actions (behaviors) create your experience in the world and ultimately what your life looks like—your results. If your thoughts suck, your life is going to suck. If you aren't conscious of your negative thoughts, you are enslaved by them. I call this the "spin cycle," as depicted in the diagram on the next page...

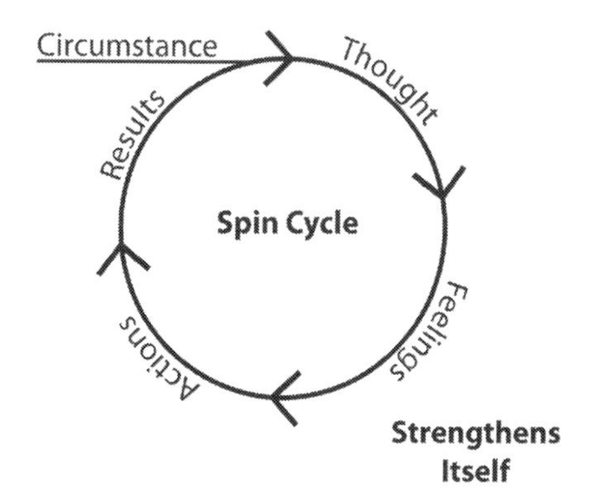

This is the negative spin cycle of thinking. The circumstance triggers the thought that gets the cycle started. The negative thought leads to the negative feeling, then action, then result. The result caused by the original thought is now evidence for the thought and strengthens its "hold" on our brain patterns—and so the spin continues to get stronger and more engrained and causes more pain.

Many coaching programs and some types of modern behavioral therapies attempt to change or "fix" the negative spin cycle and its results by changing the actions and results without changing their cause. As you can see from the diagram below, this is like swimming against the current. All this really does is cause resistance and tension. The tension seeks release and, in the case of a negative spin cycle, something has to give. Either the thought must change or the action/results must change back to their original non-tensioned cycle. When we don't change the thought (the cause), we end up back with the same spin cycle and same results over and over again.

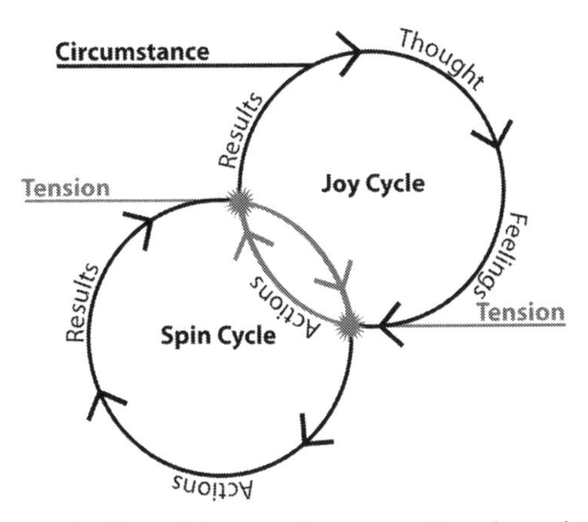

Instead of working against ourselves by taking action, using force and garnering will power as shown in the diagram above, we can become conscious of the thinking causing the unwanted results in our lives. We don't need to change the direction or result of the spin cycle—we need to consciously create an entire new pattern or cycle of thought as shown in the diagram below:

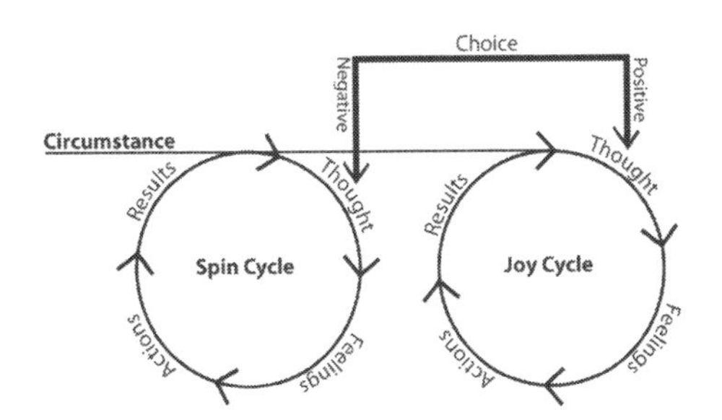

I would love to ask the people who flew the planes into the World Trade Center what thought drove that action. They believed that thought—but did they ever question the thought? Was it a thought programmed into them and accepted without inquiry? My guess is yes. What if they had looked at their left brain thought from a right brain view? What if they had become conscious that they were not their thoughts? What type of Awakened Action would have stemmed from the inquiry? What cycle of thought might they have created instead? Interesting to think about.

So, on the smaller scale of you and me, let's take a look at the results you are getting in your life. Is there anything you have or don't have that you want to change? Is there any way you are feeling that you don't want to feel—or something you want to feel more of? Well then, you picked up a book that can give you a pretty good start. And that start is with your thoughts.

Let's change your thoughts to change your results. Let's do it with the Self Coaching 101 model that is easy to understand and use. And let's keep doing it until you have the life you want, the feelings you want, the Consciousness you want.

Your thoughts determine your results and your feelings. Your thoughts are created by a Peanut chatterbox who has been running the show. It's time to take back the wheel, time to take back your mind so you can use it—instead of having it use you.

CHAPTER 1.

Model Overview

How would you feel if your husband forgot your birthday? How would you want to be able to feel? Do you realize you have complete control over how you choose to feel? Did you know that anger is just an option? Well, Sylvia didn't, when she called me for a session the day after her 45th birthday—the day her husband forgot her birthday.

In this chapter, I am going to introduce you to the model the way I introduced it to Sylvia. I will show you how I use it in my life and with my clients. This model is designed for one purpose—to change the thoughts that cause you suffering. I will start with Sylvia's example in the model to show you how to identify a negative thought and then show you a sample with the thought changed to a better feeling thought. This work was the real work I did with my client, Sylvia. Her husband had forgotten her birthday and she was seething mad. I taught her the model and showed her the way to change her thinking in order to get some relief from her pain and anger. Her actual work is shown below. Don't worry if it doesn't make complete sense the first time you see it—I am just giving you a peek. I'll go into much more detail through the rest of the book.

BAD FEELING THOUGHT SAMPLE:

Circumstance: My husband forgot my birthday.
Thought: He doesn't care about me.
Feelings: horrible, sad, lonely, angry
Action: Give him the cold shoulder and avoid him.
Result: Less time spent with husband—less caring with husband.

CHANGED THOUGHT SAMPLE:

Circumstance: My husband forgot my birthday.
Thought: I know my husband wants to help me celebrate my birthday, so I will remind him.
Feeling: Satisfied, love
Action: Connect with husband, love husband unconditionally.
Result: Enjoy my birthday with my husband.

Notice that the thoughts in the first and second samples are OPTIONAL. You get to decide what you think and you have the option of thinking something that feels terrible or thinking something that feels great. Also, notice in the changed sample that the circumstance is *exactly the same.* All the power to change how you feel is in your thinking. This is great news, because it is the one area in your life where you do have total control.

I came up with this model as a way to manage my thoughts on a daily basis. It was heavily inspired by the work of many of my teachers, especially the work of Byron Katie. I started doing The Work in my life on a daily basis about three years ago. What Katie's process did for me that was so profound, was to teach me that every time I thought something, I had a feeling associated with that thought. Her most powerful sub-question—one that I used over and over—was, "How do you feel when you think that thought?" This took me out of the idea that the thing happening in the world (the circumstance) was causing my feelings and taught me that it was the thought causing my feelings.

I did The Work for quite a while and enjoyed the relief it gave me. As I worked with my clients and continued to work on myself, I customized the way I did The Work and added the subcomponents of actions and results when I coached myself. The more I worked on this concept with myself and the more I read of Eckhart, Jill, Pema, Abraham and Martha, the more I refined this process.

The Self Coaching model is based on the following truths:

* We cannot control the world.
* Nothing outside of us has the power to make us feel good or bad.
* It is not the circumstances, but our thoughts about the circumstances that create our experience.
* We attract what we think about.
* Emotions are vibrations that lead to action.
* We can't permanently change our results without changing our thoughts.
* We don't have to get anything to feel better; we can feel better right now.
* Being conscious and choosing our thoughts are the most important components to feeling better.

Here are the reasons to use this model daily:

- ✔ To feel better
- ✔ To create results
- ✔ To become conscious
- ✔ To think more deliberately
- ✔ To create/manifest what you want in your life
- ✔ To remove negative thinking and emotions
- ✔ To create positive thinking and emotions

So go ahead and take a look at the model below. This is the tool in its entirety.

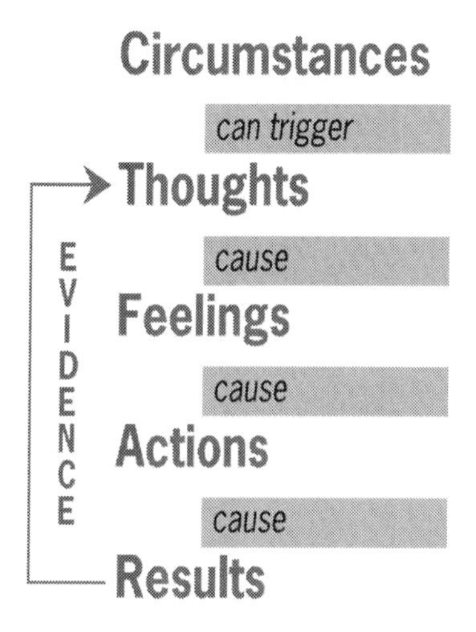

Here are the terms the way I define them:

Circumstances: Things that happen in the world that we cannot control.

Thoughts: Things that happen in your mind. This is where you self coach.

Feelings: Vibrations that happen in your body—caused by thoughts, not circumstances.

Actions: Behavior—what we do in the world. Caused by feelings, determined by thought.

Results: What we see in the world (our lives) as an effect of our actions. The result will always be evidence for the original thought.

As you use this model and work on your thoughts, you will assume the position of the Watcher. Doing this work is the best way to get out of your socially programmed thought patterns and identify with a deeper level of consciousness. As the Watcher, you become more and more aware of who you really are—someone who is not at the mercy of unconscious thinking. Realizing that every feeling, action, and result you create in your life is because of a thought is life altering. Notice this truth and fill in the main worksheet (p. 38) whenever you have a negative thought, feeling, action, or result. The mere process of being Aware of these components in your life is enough to change your life. Identifying with the part of you that observes your thinking is aligning with your Source Energy (Abraham), Compassionate Witness (Katie and Pema), Essential Self (Martha), Watcher, or Consciousness.

To further demonstrate this model, let me show you an example:

What is your current problem?

Answer this question without thinking too hard about it. Just write down your answer. It might look something like one of the problems listed below:

I have no meaning in my life.
I am sick and tired of this.
I am sad.
My father is dying.
I hate my job.
I weigh 275 pounds.
I keep yelling at my kids.
I drink five glasses of wine a night.
George Bush is president.
I am ugly.
I don't have enough money.
I have $20K to my name.
I am stressed about my job.

Once you have written down the problem—no matter how petty it might seem—you can categorize it into one of the five areas on the diagram.

For example: I am sad.

This is a feeling, so you would put *sad* next to "feeling" on the diagram, like this:

Circumstance
Thought
Feeling SAD
Action
Result

From here you can fill out the rest of the diagram by asking the following questions:

What is the thought causing me to feel sad?
How do I act when I feel sad?
What is the ultimate result when I feel sad?

The same applies if you use a thought, for example: *I hate my job.*

Here you would put this thought next to thought on the diagram and then ask the following questions:

Circumstance
Thought I HATE MY JOB
Feeling
Action
Result

How do I feel when I think this thought?
How do I act when I think this thought?
What is the result in my life when I think this thought?

Here is a sample that a client filled out based on starting with a circumstance in her life:

CIRCUMSTANCE **She did not show up on time.**
THOUGHT She does not respect me.
FEELING Angry, sad, rejected
ACTION Act passive aggressive. Make snide comments
RESULT Less respect from her.
(The result will always be evidence for the original thought.)

The circumstance is: She did not show up on time for a lunch date. The thought this triggered was: She does not respect me. When I think this thought, I feel angry, sad, and rejected. I act in a way that is passive aggressive and snide towards her. This gives me the ultimate result of loss of respect in my relationship with her, which proves the original thought: she doesn't respect me.

An alternate thought concerning the same issue will cause different feelings and therefore different results.

Circumstance: **She did not show up on time.**
Thoughts: She must be busy—I won't take it personally.
Feelings: Appreciative she made it, relaxed
Actions: Act kind and understanding.
Results: No effect personally—no negativity.

Here again, it is the exact same circumstance creating a different experience based on the thinking. If, when my friend shows up late, I choose to think I'm just so happy to see her (if that is believable to me) no matter that she is late—the feeling is happy and excited and the action is to engage with my friend. The result may be that we have a wonderful and respectful lunch. You can use this model to understand almost anything that is going on with you.

I will repeat this many times over the course of the book, but it is life changing to remember: IT IS NEVER THE CIRCUMSTANCE CAUSING YOUR FEELINGS—IT IS ALWAYS YOUR THINKING ABOUT THE CIRCUMSTANCE.

When you become the Watcher, or a student of yourself, you have understood the power of self coaching. You cannot be the Watcher of your thoughts and also be your thoughts at the same time. When you shine a light on the thoughts in your mind and step out of yourself, you can see that you are not what you do, what you think, your results, or your body.

The part of you that is the Watcher is the part of you that is connected to all other human beings and all other energies. When you tap into the part of you that is not the part of you reacting to emotions, you have tapped into the part of you that is powerful beyond measure.

Become the Watcher as often as possible. See yourself from a compassionate, remote perspective. Look at everything you do in your life with fascination and curiosity. Do not judge your actions or your thoughts but notice them. Just be in the noticing.

Use the model as a way to learn about your social self (your ego) and as Eckhart would say, "Learn what you are not." The thoughts in your mind are not the whole of who you are. We are what is left when we can separate who we are from the thoughts, emotions, actions, and results. We are the unchangeable force behind it all.

Here is the process again, in its entirety using the original example at the beginning of the chapter. You start with a blank model as shown here:

Circumstance: ______________________
Thought: ______________________
Feeling: ______________________
Action: ______________________
Result: ______________________

To begin the process follow the steps outlined below:

Step 1: Name your "problem" or "issue".
Step 2: Categorize it into either a circumstance, thought, feeling, action/behavior, or result.
Step 3: Fill in the rest of the model.
Step 4: Change the thought that is not working and choose a new thought.
Step 5: Put the new thought in a blank model and fill in the rest with new details.

In the example at the beginning of the chapter, we took a negative emotion and found the thought causing it, as noted here:

Circumstance: My husband forgot my birthday.
Thought: **He doesn't care about me.**
Feelings: horrible, sad, lonely
Action: Give him the cold shoulder and avoid him.
Result: Less time spent with husband—less caring with husband.

Just filling in one model, and becoming aware of what is causing you to feel bad, is enough to help you feel a bit better right now. As you do more and more of these, you will notice how much negative thinking you may be doing on a daily basis. As you move deeper into this work, you may want to delve even deeper into choosing your thoughts and deciding what you want to think. You can consciously decide to control your thoughts. If, for example, you had just completed the above model and had become more aware of what you are thinking, then you could decide what you would rather be feeling. So let's say you decide you want to feel happy because it is your birthday. You would start a new model as shown below:

Circumstance: My husband forgot my birthday.
Thought:
Feeling: Happy
Action:
Result:

From here you can ask yourself, *"What would I have to think (and truly believe) in this situation in order to feel happy?"* Some possible thoughts might be: *My husband loves me. My husband wants to celebrate with me. My husband is so much fun and will be excited when I remind him it is my birthday.* Pick one, see if it creates the feeling of happy that you are looking for, and then add it to the model.

Circumstance: My husband forgot my birthday.
Thought: My husband wants to celebrate with me.
Feeling: Happy
Action:
Result:

This is not wishful thinking. This is not psychobabble. This is you choosing what you think. This is you deciding there is no upside to feeling badly about this. There is no upside in trying to make him feel bad about forgetting.

Once you have the thought that you genuinely believe and it brings you a feeling of happiness (the original feeling you were seeking), you can fill in the action section by asking yourself what action you might take when you feel happy.

Circumstance: My husband forgot my birthday.
Thought: My husband wants to celebrate with me.
Feeling: Happy
Action: Connect with husband by reminding him and celebrating with him.
Result:

The final step is to ask yourself what result that action will create and fill in the final portion of the model.

Circumstance: My husband forgot my birthday.
Thought: My husband wants to celebrate with me.
Feeling: Happy
Action: Connect with husband by reminding him and celebrating with him.
Result: Enjoy my birthday with my husband.

Start with a happy feeling, and you will take a happy action, which leads to a happy result. Seem too simple? Seem a bit silly? Try it out. It has completely changed my life.

In the next five chapters, I will go into a deeper explanation of each of the parts of the model with this general overview as a guide. We will explore each component and how they work in relation to each other. The power of this process is in first recognizing the thinking that you may not be aware of and understanding how you are creating your own experience with your thinking. After identifying the thoughts that aren't working, you can then consciously decide on your own terms what you will choose to think. All those negative thoughts, created by that small peanut-sized area in your brain, are running around like wild animals, and can be understood, acknowledged, corralled, released, and/or changed.

To get started, try filling out the following worksheet to get a general feel for the process. Identify your problem as a thought, feeling, result, or behavior, and plug it into the model. Fill in the rest of the model. Then give a try at a better feeling thought. It might feel awkward and bit confusing in the beginning, but as we go through the book it will get easier. Don't over-think the process; just fill in the form with what comes to mind. There is a copy of this main worksheet at the end of the book if you want to make copies.

SELF COACHING 101 MAIN WORKSHEET

UNINTENTIONAL THOUGHT PATTERN

CIRCUMSTANCE: ______________________________

____

____

THOUGHT: ______________________________

____

____

FEELING: ______________________________

____

____

ACTION: ______________________________

____

____

RESULT: ______________________________

____

INTENTIONAL THOUGHT PATTERN

CIRCUMSTANCE: ______________________________

____

____

NEW THOUGHT: ______________________________

____

____

FEELING: ______________________________

____

____

ACTION: ______________________________

____

____

RESULT: ______________________________

____

CHAPTER 2

Model in Detail:

CIRCUMSTANCES

"The things we can't control."

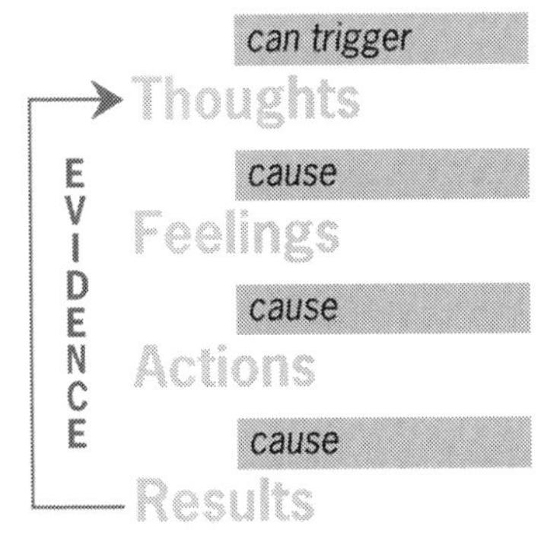

Janet hates her boss. He is controlling and arrogant, and thinks he is better than her. He diminishes her accomplishments and exaggerates her mistakes. She feels trapped by him because she has to keep the job to keep food on the table. Every day she goes to work filled with dread and the secret wish to quit her job. She hired me to help her in picking a new career path. On our first call, she spent the first 30 minutes in a very convincing rant about her boss. I would title the drama she relayed as "My Boss is the Devil." As she continued, I asked her, "If your boss is the devil, what does that make you?"

"What do you mean?" she asked. "I am not making this up. These aren't just thoughts I am having. He really does act this way."

"I believe you," I said, "and so what?"

"Well, easy for you to say, Brooke. You don't have to work for him every day. This guy really is a nightmare."

"Working for your boss is your circumstance, Janet. Your circumstance is not causing this pain; your thoughts about this circumstance are what throw you into suffering," I told her.

"Whatever," she said with doubt and resignation.

There was a brief silence on the phone and then she continued, "Brooke, I think it is naïve of you to say that my boss, who I work with everyday of my life, has no control over my mood."

"I hear that you don't believe me and yet what I am telling you is the truth. Let's explore this more deeply. Tell me something your boss said to you yesterday that you believe affected your mood."

"Okay, so we went to a meeting yesterday and he asked for an update on my progress on a project that is ongoing. When I started to speak, he rudely interrupted me and said, 'Janet, we don't need a full dissertation on what you have done; we just need an update on where you are now.' I felt totally humiliated."

This is when I jumped into the model with her. I showed her that the **circumstance** was her boss saying:

"Janet, we don't need a full dissertation on what you have done; we just need an update on where you are now." I then asked her what her **thought** was about what her boss said. She said, "What do you think my thought was? It was: *My boss is such a jerk and he just made me look like a loser in front of my entire team.*" Janet said this to me like it was obvious. She stated this thought like it was a given and that anyone would have had the same thought. I pointed out to her that this was not the case. I showed her that this thought is the cause of her humiliation, not what her boss said.

She could have just as easily thought, "My boss is in a hurry today and needs me to be concise and I can do that. This is not a reflection on me, but on him." This thought would have left her feeling efficient instead of humiliated.

Knowing the difference between a thought and a circumstance can change how you feel in any moment, as it did for Janet. Throughout this book, I am going to go into detail for each term on the model. The first term is circumstances. Briefly, I define this term as things that happen in the world. Circumstances are the things that we don't have direct control over from our current position.

Now, the Law of Attraction and Abraham would say that we do have control over the circumstances we attract into our lives, and that everything we experience is because of our current vibration. With this law, we would need to say that every circumstance is actually a result we have created, and there is some truth to this, as you will see later in this book. But for the sake of simplicity, we are going to keep the terms separate, and call circumstances the things in the world we can't personally or *directly* control right now. An example of circumstances in the world might include other people's behavior, the weather, the political climate, war, death, taxes, other people's illnesses, the mortgage crisis, others' opinion of us, the past, and child abuse. There are, of course, many more.

As Katie would say, "Circumstances are reality and when you argue with reality you lose, but only 100% of the time." What Katie means by this is that it is not the circumstance that is causing us pain, but rather our thoughts about it, our argument against it, that causes us pain. No matter how horrific your past, no matter how horrible the event, the only thing that ever causes us emotional pain is our story (thoughts) about it.

I must note, that accepting the things we cannot change is one of the most powerful things we can do. It seems almost paradoxical to think of acceptance as a powerful action. Many of my clients believe that if they accept reality they lose all their power to ever change it—but this is simply not true. Accepting the present moment exactly the way it is now, without completely identifying with it, is where all our power is. Eckhart tells us over and over that the only power we have is in the moment we have right now. When we are spending our present moment in a fight we cannot win (arguing with reality), we are always losing our present moment.

That being said, there is a huge difference between accepting and condoning. Accepting the way things are does not mean we agree with them or condone them. It just means we are not trying to change something by pushing hard against it. We are choosing not to go to war. We are choosing not to try and force change with our own negative feelings. We can act from a place of peace and love and still move towards change. There is so much freedom when we release resistance against what the circumstances are. This does not disempower us. Just because we are not fighting or hating (which feels awful) does not mean we can't be an agent of change in the world. In fact, the opposite is true. Freedom from the fight in our mind is where we must begin if we want freedom in the world.

Let me give you an example. Let's say your mother beat you physically when you were a child and you cannot accept it. You may have built up an identity around this. You may see yourself as a victim. In this present moment, some 40 years later, you are no longer being physically harmed by your mother. The only pain still associated with that event is your current thinking. If you are constantly arguing with the past by thinking thoughts like, *"She should have been a better mother. She should have loved me. How could she have done that to me? I hate her. If she hadn't done that, I wouldn't be so messed up,"* etc., you are in a place of non-acceptance. Each one of those thoughts causes tremendous pain right now in the present. She is no longer causing you physical pain, but you continue the pain by fighting against the past and reliving the emotional pain in your mind.

So to be very clear: Right now, what is painful about your past is your current thought. Period. I am sorry your mother beat you. Truly. But I am sorrier that you continue to beat yourself with your current thoughts. This does not mean it is okay that your mother beat you. I would never condone physical harm as an appropriate action. But that is a circumstance we cannot change. What we can change is how you think about it. We can change every thought you have about that experience into a thought that does not cause you pain. In this way, we can literally change your feelings about the past. Accept that your mother beat you. Stop arguing with it. This does not mean that you agree with her behavior or condone her actions, it means you can accept it and let it go. In this way, you stop the beatings.

The most common and arguably the most painful circumstances we cannot change are other people's behavior. We sure would like to, though. My clients and I have thick manuals of how we want our husbands, kids, and friends to behave. And they never follow them! If only they would read my manual and follow it, I would be so happy. But they never do. When we think that people should be different than they are, we cause ourselves so much misery. We think thoughts like, "They should be kinder. They shouldn't kill. They shouldn't hit. They shouldn't be mean. They should do their homework. They should pay attention. They should be more affectionate. They should...(fill in the blank)." As Katie would say, "Hopeless." Trying to change that which we cannot control is painful. It also puts us in a place of complete powerlessness.

Circumstances are neutral. They don't cause pain. Three dollars in the bank when you want $200k is still just three dollars. It doesn't cause pain. It just sits in the bank. One hundred extra pounds on your body is just tissue. It just sits there. It isn't personal. It doesn't "hate" you. It just neutrally exists. Scales aren't evil—they are a piece of metal. People don't say mean things to you because of you; they say mean things to you because of *them*. When Jill went through her ordeal after the stroke, she didn't care what people thought of her. With her inability to concoct a story about others' behavior being about her, she clearly saw it as their own. It released her from the pain of her thoughts about it. Katie walks into a room and thinks to herself, "They all love me. I just don't expect them to know it yet." Now that is a brilliantly chosen thought! It's a thought that feels good, no matter how other people behave.

The other interesting thing about circumstances is that there are so many of them! You can look into your life and see so many people, places and things: neutral things, waiting for your mind to judge them. How we think about the world is what creates our experience of it. If we look at a tree and marvel at its beauty, we will feel wonderful. If we look at tree and think about how it blocks our view, we will feel terrible. Same circumstance, different thought, and therefore a different feeling.

Another example I like to use in my seminars is the winning lottery ticket. If I give you a winning lottery ticket and you believe that you have just won 10 million dollars, how will you feel about it? Most of my clients say, "Elated. Stoked. Excited. Pumped." What caused these feelings? The winning lottery ticket? The money in their bank when they cash it in? No. The winning lottery ticket is neutral. It is literally a piece of paper that causes nothing. It is all the thinking that is associated with that ticket that causes the elation. Thoughts like, "I am rich. I am so lucky. I will buy a new house, car, and boat. I will never have to worry about money again. I can buy whatever I want." Those thoughts are what have the power to create so much positive emotion in the present moment.

Now, what if I tell you that I was just kidding and that isn't the winning ticket after all? Does that make the emotion you just experienced less real? Does it take away the elation vibration you just experienced? Does it mean you were never happy? No. What now changes the emotion are all your new thoughts. If you are feeling a negative emotion at this point it may be because you are thinking thoughts like, "I knew it was too good to be true. I am so unlucky. I can't stand this stupid seminar. That was mean."

Has the lottery circumstance changed? No. You still haven't won the lottery. You never had. But with your thoughts you went from elation to depression in a matter of minutes. And even if you had won the lottery, it wouldn't be the lottery that causes your happiness about it. It would be your thoughts. Even with the money in your bank (circumstance), the only joy you will ever feel because of that money is because of the thoughts you think about it.

Let circumstances be. You don't have a choice anyway. People do what they do, our past is what it is, our weight is what it is right now and our bank account is what it is. This doesn't mean it won't change, but arguing with it now has no upside. Arguing with reality is just thinking negative, untrue thoughts that serve no purpose but pain.

Whenever you explain your current feeling state based on something that "happened" you are missing the middleman, which is your thinking. Following are some samples of self coaching from clients who presented with what they thought were terrible circumstances.

Five different circumstances:

- ✎ My son just got expelled from school for using drugs.
- ✎ My sister told my husband he could do better.
- ✎ My mother insists on coming to my house for Christmas.
- ✎ I don't have enough money to pay my bills.
- ✎ My weight is 100 lbs over my natural weight right now.

Here is their work:

Circumstance: **My son just got expelled from school for using drugs.**
Thought: I am a terrible mom and didn't do a good job raising him.
Feelings: inadequate, sad, frustrated
Action: Cry, argue with the principal, speak harshly to my son.
Result: Everyone responds defensively and I end up in a fight with the principal and my son.

Circumstance: **My sister told my husband he could do better.**
Thought: My sister is such a bitch. She doesn't love me.
Feelings: angry, sad, embarrassed, betrayed
Action: Talk to my husband about how much I hate my sister. Give my sister the cold shoulder.
Result: My sister feels even more convinced that my husband could do better. I am less close with my sister.

Circumstance: **My mother insists on coming to my house for Christmas.**
Thought: I have to let her come because she is my mother.
Feeling: Resentful
Action: I tell my mom she can come and then I act like a complete whiny child while she is here.
Result: My mom treats me like a child and continues to tell me what to do.

Circumstance: **I don't have enough money to pay my bills.**
Thought: I am going to have to foreclose on my home.
Feeling: horrible, depressed, sad, defeated
Action: Lie on the couch most the day and eat instead of looking for work.
Result: No second job and no more money to pay the bills.

Circumstance: **My weight is 100 lbs over my natural weight right now.**
Thought: There is something wrong with me and I have no self-control.
Feeling: Defeated
Action: Eat in order not to feel.
Result: I gain more weight.

Notice that in all the examples, the result provides additional evidence for the thought. The mind is seeking and creating evidence for its own thinking even though it is very painful. Also, it is important to note that for the sake of this model, when you start with a painful thought (not a circumstance as in the above cases) or a feeling, action, or result, you do not need to fill in the circumstance that triggered the thought. At that point it is irrelevant. It is the thought about the circumstance that we are after because we can change our thinking and our thinking will change our feelings, actions, and results.

Here is a sample:

Circumstance:
Thought: My husband isn't attentive.
Feeling: frustrated, lonely
Action: Act cold toward him.
Result: Less attention and less connection.

In this case the client presented with the thought, and understanding the circumstance was not important. As a coach, many of my clients really want to tell me the circumstance and give me all the details. I usually try to stop them from doing this because what they are really doing is building their evidence for the thought that is causing them pain. "My husband isn't attentive. He came home from work and didn't even say hello. Then, I came out with a new dress on, and he didn't even notice. He watches sports much more than he talks to me." These are the circumstances that she ultimately cannot control. She can only control her thoughts about it—so that is where we begin.

A question that I often get is, "What is the difference between a circumstance and a result?" The difference in relation to this model is that a circumstance is something you cannot directly control *in this moment.*

To use the example above, you can see that your current result may become your next circumstance. The result may be a weight gain after the action of overeating. This weight gain now is your circumstance because it is not something you can change in this moment—the only thing you can change in this moment is your thinking about your weight. So you can see how the models can stack in this way:

Circumstance: My weight is 100lbs over my natural weight right now.
Thought: There is something wrong with me and I have no self-control.
Feeling: Defeated
Action: Eat in order not to feel.
Result: I gain more weight.

New Circumstance: My weight is 102lbs over my natural weight right now.

Your results can create new circumstances in your life but they are not circumstances in and of themselves. Circumstances may be the current effect of a result or they may have absolutely nothing to do with you at all. Remember that circumstances are things you cannot control or change *in this moment.*

When I was first creating this model, one of my best challenges on it came from one of my clients. She said, "So what about my messy house? Is that a circumstance or a result? I do have control over it and I can change it." I replied, "First, your statement that your house is messy is really a thought about the state of your house—but I see where you are going with your question, so let's just restate it for clarity. You can say, "My house is not as clean as it usually is." This is more factual vs. judgmental, because the word messy is relative. So, you have a house that is not as clean as usual and you wonder if it is a circumstance because you feel you do have the ability to control it by, say, cleaning it. Here is where the "in this moment" piece becomes important. You do not have direct control in this moment to completely change the circumstance of the unclean house. And yes, the unclean house may have been a result of another thought you had earlier in the week, but it is still your current circumstance in this moment. Here is the model work on it:

Circumstance: An unclean house
Thought: I have to get a grip—I can't even keep my own house in order.
Feeling: Frustrated , angry, embarrassed
Action: Clean the house while I beat myself up.
Result: A clean house and a defeated sense of myself.

Alternative

Circumstance: An unclean house
Thought: I have time to clean my house now and I am good at it.
Feeling: energized and confident
Action: Clean the house and listen to great music.
Result: A clean house and an appreciation of my work.

Remember, this model is used when you are suffering. It is a tool that works when we are suffering because of our thinking. We do not use this model when we are dealing with thoughts and circumstances that do not cause prolonged suffering because it would not be useful. Here is an example of a circumstance where the model would not be useful, and there are many more like it.

> Circumstance: There is a bug in my eye.
> Thought: I am going to take the bug out of my eye.
> Feeling: Confident in my abilities
> Action: Take the bug out of my eye.
> Result: No bug in my eye (notice it proves the original thought).

As you can see, this work was unnecessary. Even though the circumstance was not ideal, the thought never went to negativity so the relief happened quickly. There are many examples like this where doing the model would be redundant and unnecessary. Use the model when the circumstance/thinking pattern is causing you to suffer and you cannot access immediate relief. We do not need to use the model when we are feeling good about something. Feelings in this model are not feelings of physical or involuntary pain, but rather our emotional feelings caused by our thoughts. You notice that I did not include the physical discomfort caused by the bug because it does not fall under the definition of feeling in this model.

I think I covered all the bases on circumstances, and I don't want to make this more complicated than it has to be. It really is simple if you don't over-think it and you go with the general definition of circumstances being things you cannot control now. You'll know you need to use the model when you are suffering and you believe it is because of an external circumstance of your life. Use the following worksheet with the model and write the circumstance at the top and then fill in the model. The most important thing to know is that it is your thinking—not your circumstances—that causes all your suffering.

WHEN THE PROBLEM SEEMS TO BE A CIRCUMSTANCE

What is the circumstance? ____________________________________

____

____

What thought does the circumstance trigger? ____________________

____

____

____

What do you feel when you think this thought? __________________

____

____

____

How do you act when you feel this way? ________________________

____

____

____

What is the result of this action? ______________________________

____

____

____

How does the result prove the original thought? __________________

____

____

____

What is a better feeling thought to choose concerning this circumstance? ____

____

____

Use the questions above to fill in the unintentional thought patterns.

UNINTENTIONAL THOUGHT PATTERN

CIRCUMSTANCE: ____

____

____

THOUGHT: ____

____

____

FEELING: ____

____

____

ACTION: ____

____

____

RESULT: ____

____

____

INTENTIONAL THOUGHT PATTERN

CIRCUMSTANCE: ____

____

____

NEW THOUGHT: ____

____

____

FEELING: ____

____

____

ACTION: ____

____

____

RESULT: ____

____

____

Notes:

CHAPTER 3

Model in Detail:

THOUGHTS

"A sentence formed in our mind."

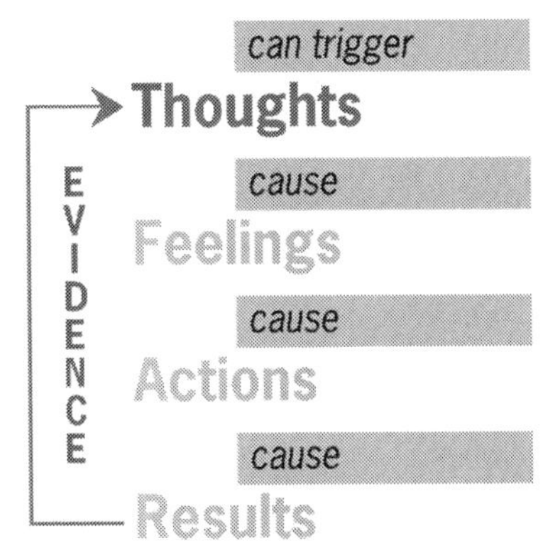

Without her left hemisphere thinking judgmental thoughts, Jill was happy. She didn't care that she was drooling, that she didn't know what a number was, or that she was a Harvard trained PhD. She was a former brain scientist who couldn't do a child's puzzle, and yet she was peaceful and joyous.

Her chatter-box Peanut was choking on the blood from a stroke and didn't have a chance to tell her that this was "terrible." So she smiled and drooled on the couch in a state of perfect peace. She was at one with the universe and she couldn't make her own breakfast.

This is not to say that she didn't want to ever think again. She saw the value of her left hemisphere's language center and consciously made the effort to regain the part of her thinking mind that was useful to her. She also chose not to reengage the part of her Peanut that was harshly judgmental, worried incessantly, or was verbally abusive to others. She realized, by the temporary absence of those thoughts, how good she felt not having them. So she chose not to think those thoughts anymore. She chose not to reintroduce the neurological circuitry that ran the loops of worry, judgment, and pain.

If we don't play our circuitry of doom, we don't feel the negative emotion it causes. If we manage what we think about and question our thoughts, we rewire our habits of thought. We literally change the pathways inside our brain. But just like any habit, if your brain is running on automatic pilot (and you haven't had a stroke), you have to become aware and disciplined in witnessing your thoughts—instead of letting your mind run the show. Instead of letting Peanut determine what you will manifest and feel, take back that power and start consciously and deliberately deciding what to think.

How do you know if you should question or change a thought? IF YOU DON'T LIKE THE WAY IT MAKES YOU FEEL. There is no need to question thoughts that feel good. Good feelings lead to good actions which lead to good results. Question any thought that doesn't give you the feeling, action, or result you want.

Remember that most thoughts that cause pain are not true. Just because a thought you are thinking feels true doesn't mean it is true. Your feelings are the *effect of your thinking*—not evidence that your thinking is true.

Also, keep in mind the last chapter which discussed the difference between a circumstance (fact) and a thought as we do this work on thoughts. A circumstance is something you do not have any direct control over in this moment; but your thoughts are completely within your control. For example, your mother dying is a circumstance, but thinking that she is dying too early is a thought. Circumstances do not cause feelings—only our thoughts cause feelings.

There are many ways to change a thought—but I am going to teach you the easiest and quickest way I know. If you want to become a Master at changing your thinking, please go to www.thework.com. Byron Katie is by far the best teacher for changing thinking on the planet.

Here is my shortened, quick-start version of thought changing:

- Write down the painful thought.
- Write down the feeling the thought causes you to feel.
- Write down a slightly better feeling thought that you know is true.
- Write down the feeling the new thought causes you to feel.
- Repeat as needed.

Example:

Original thought: **I am fat and ugly.** (ashamed)

Replacement thoughts:

I have nice lips. (happy)
I have pretty hair. (proud)
I am kind. (content)
I am not as fat as I used to be. (glad)

Byron Katie will take you to a full turnaround after asking four other questions, and this can be incredibly powerful. My quick-start process has you inch up the chain by finding a better feeling thought that you can already believe in completely. This combines the work of Esther Hicks, Byron Katie, and Pema Chodron. I have found this process to be indescribably helpful in dealing with any negative emotion.

After you change the thought, plug it into the model and fully integrate what it would mean for you to focus on it. When you are picking a new thought, make sure it is a thought you genuinely believe and that it will lead to a good feeling. You might want to ask yourself how you want to feel and then you can ask what thought would create that feeling.

"Thought appears," as Katie and Pema would say. There is not a darn thing we can do about that. The brain runs and does its job and creates mind noise. The question is: Are we paying attention? Are we conscious of what we are thinking? Or are we just la la la acting out our thoughts with complete lack of knowing or awareness? Are we attaching to negative loops of circuitry and believing lies? Are we unconsciously letting Peanut take us on the train of suffering and pretending we don't have a choice?

Wanna know what your brain circuitry loops look like? What they are saying? Take a look at your life. Those results you have in your life are because of the thoughts you have in your head. No money? You have no-abundant-money thought circuitry. Overweight? Overweight thought circuitry. Bored? Bored thought circuitry.

Great. Some of you are looking at your life right now and creating even deeper, stronger ruts of circuitry that say, "I am not good enough." PAY ATTENTION.

Just by noticing these thoughts from a Watcher perspective, you are changing the pattern. You are creating what Jill might call a "right brain" perspective. Eckhart would be so pleased that you are becoming more awakened in this present moment. You have transcended thought just by becoming conscious of it. TRANSCENDENCE! You cannot be your thought and be conscious of your thought at the same time. Consciousness of the ego dissolves the ego. Enlightenment is not knowing *about* you—it is being you. When you are watching your mind you are **being** in the place of the Watcher, The Knowing, The Awareness, and that is Enlightenment.

So first, before you get all action-stepped on me and ask how the heck to continue to change your thoughts, stay with this truth for a minute. Just by being aware of your thoughts, you have changed so much. Just by identifying with the right brain, the consciousness, the hemisphere where Peanut is not allowed in the house:

You have become enlightened, according to Eckhart.
You have arrived in the present moment by not attaching to thought, according to Pema.
You have become aware of what you have been asking-for, according to Abraham.
You have become the Stargazer, according to Martha.
And you have "entered the only dimension where you do have some control," according to Katie.
Tony would remind you that you have just witnessed the best money-making tool in the Universe—your thoughts.

Becoming Conscious of your thoughts is step 1 and—even though there are 5 more steps—if you get through step 1 you are more than half-way there. Become aware of what you are thinking. Take full responsibility for what thoughts you attach to. Remember that a belief is just a thought you keep on thinking, or a thought that has a tremendous amount of emotion associated with it. Remember that your entire identity and how you "see" yourself is all from your "mind's eye" or more accurately, your mind's thoughts. Looking at your mind instead of being in your mind is the key.

Take a moment right now and go into the watcher. Pay attention to the first 10 thoughts you think and write them here:

1. ______________________________
2. ______________________________
3. ______________________________
4. ______________________________
5. ______________________________
6 ______________________________

7. ____________________________________
8. ____________________________________
9 ____________________________________
10. ____________________________________

By doing this exercise you are more enlightened, just by being aware of your thoughts. I am also going to assume that much of what you wrote is not to your liking. Most likely you are having many thoughts that cause you to feel, well, crappy. So this is where I think Eckhart leaves us hanging a bit. He tells us to be in the present moment and watch our thoughts which I think is easy to say because he doesn't really have any negative thoughts since waking up to Nirvana that one beautiful day in July. The rest of us become conscious of our thoughts and see that there is a really frickin good reason we have stayed unconscious all these years. It is a war zone in there. Not many pretty things to see.

Here is a sampling from my mind and the minds of some of my clients:

I am not good enough.
I am ugly.
Look at those wrinkles.
Does Botox really work?
Do you think she would ever sleep with me?
I must do something for approval.
My boss hates me.
He makes more money than me.
I am not enough.
Seriously, do you think she would sleep with me if I wasn't married?
No one loves me enough.

His parents were rich—that is why he got that job.
I need more money.
I think my wife is heavier than her.
I am a victim.
My father will never be proud of me.
My mother never shuts up.
My hair is stringy.
Fat is hanging over my pants.
I wonder if I got her drunk...that might work.
How did I end up in this life that sucks so badly?
I don't have enough time.
There is never going to be enough.
I haven't saved for my kids' college fund.
How the hell can he afford that car?
Do I have enough time to get her drunk and sleep with her?
I need lipo.

So, we witness our thoughts and see something like this and we are supposed to think we are Awakened? I wonder what Eckhart would think of this Present moment Awareness? The truth is, he would nod quietly, love unconditionally, and note that the ego is a busy little peanut. Then, he would remind us to breathe.

Are you like me? Do you skip that "take a breath" part? I just want to get onto the not-feeling-pain part. I want to get on to the thinking-thoughts-that-make-me-skinny-and-rich part. The breathing part seems to delay the result part. Why, Pema? Why, Eckhart? Why breathe, again? Talk me into it.

Breathing brings us to the present moment.

But what if I don't want this present moment? What if I want a future moment where I am skinny and rich? Eckhart would tell me that the only way to get there is from here. Pema would tell me to release my attachment to the idea that skinny and rich is where peace resides. Katie would ask me to question that thought. Tony would ask me why the heck I wasn't rich already. And he would have a point. And the answer to his question would be that I have a belief in this moment that I can't have it and there will never be enough. And as long as I believe that in this moment, I can't move towards having it in a future moment. Abraham would say it is LAW. You can't attract something you are not aligned with and as long as I am thinking I can't be rich, or skinny or whatever, I won't ever be.

Breathing in the present moment makes this all clear. Breathing in the present moment with consciousness is where any painful thought is dissolved.

At this point, you can use Katie's inquiry to turn the thought around, or Abraham's suggestion to find a better feeling thought or Tony's process of programming the mind to associate massive pain with the thought so you won't think it again. Pema would remind us not to attach to or fight the thought, but to just be at peace with it and have a look.

I, personally, do Katie's work on the really painful thoughts. I have never found anything more effective for feeling a tremendous wave of relief than taking a painful thought, asking her four questions, and doing a turn around. For the smaller thoughts, I use the process I described earlier in this chapter of finding a better feeling thought and focusing my mind on what

I want in my life. Most often, just by becoming aware of the thought and by giving it the light of awareness, it disappears. I am not sure if it is because of practice or because my brain has rewired, but I do know that the more I practice this, the more it works.

A thought is a thing. A statement. A collection of words. It is the cause of your feelings. It is the cause of what you manifest. It is the basis for belief systems and it is what determines your attraction. It is run by a little group of cells the size of a peanut. It is our job to use the rest of our brain to manage that little peanut because, although it is a very important piece of our life, it is not management material. The little mind, the ego, the cause of what Jill calls "internal self-abuse," is the cause of more misery on the planet than everything else combined. Peanut chatter starts wars and justifies abuse. It needs supervision and the supervisor is YOU.

Start now by filling out the following worksheets on one negative thought. Then, do it on any remaining negative thoughts. Don't stop until you feel good.

FINDING A NEW THOUGHT

What is your current painful thought? ______________________________

____

____

Why are you choosing to believe it? ______________________________

____

____

____

Is there any part of this thought that is not factual? ________________

____

____

What part of this thought is your opinion? __________________________

____

____

Can you imagine someone else having this exact thought with a different opinion?______On a scale of 1-10 how important is this thought?____How big is this thought? The size of a penny? A bread-box? A building?____

How can you make this thought smaller? ___________________________

____

____

What would you say to a small child thinking this thought?__________

____

____

Write down three better feeling thoughts that that you truly believe.

1. ____

____

____

2. ____

____

3. ______________________________

____

When you plug this new thought into the self coaching model, what changes? ______________________________

____

____

____

____

What is funny about the original thought? (Find something, anything.)

____

____

____

____

How would your life change if you changed this one thought? ______

____

____

____

____

What is the new thought? ______________________________

____

____

____

Rewrite the thought until you truly believe it. ______________________________

____

____

____

____

____

____

____

____

THOUGHT PROBLEM WORKSHEET

What is the negative **thought** you keep thinking? ________________

____

____

____

What **feeling** does this thought cause you? ________________

____

____

____

How do you **behave** when you feel this way? ________________

____

____

____

What is the **result** of this action? ________________

____

____

____

____

How does the result prove the original thought? ________________

____

____

____

____

What is a better **feeling** thought to think that is believable to you? ____

____

____

____

Use the questions above to fill in
the unintentional thought patterns.

UNINTENTIONAL THOUGHT PATTERN

CIRCUMSTANCE: ______________________________

____

____

THOUGHT: ______________________________

____

____

FEELING: ______________________________

____

____

ACTION: ______________________________

____

____

RESULT: ______________________________

____

____

INTENTIONAL THOUGHT PATTERN

CIRCUMSTANCE: ______________________________

____

____

NEW THOUGHT: ______________________________

____

____

FEELING: ______________________________

____

____

ACTION: ______________________________

____

____

RESULT: ______________________________

____

____

CHAPTER 4

Model in Detail:

FEELINGS

"A vibration in our bodies caused by our mind."

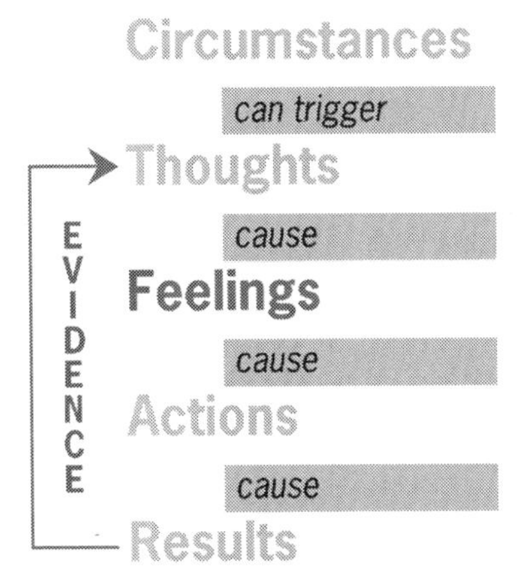

It is all about feelings. Really, that is the whole reason we do anything. We feel good and we associate good feelings with it and so we do more of it. How we feel determines what we do and what we don't do. So what really are these things we call feelings that we spend so much time avoiding and seeking?

The definition on the web of a feeling is: Feelings are the emotional state of mind which can't be explained but only experienced.

I like this definition. I like that it shows that feelings are an effect of the mind—experienced in our body.

It is very important to note that when I am talking about feelings here I am only referring to feelings that are the effect of the mind and not physical sensations that are caused by the body or external environment directly. I am not including illness, physical conditions like being cold or hot, hunger, physical pain, the startle reflex, fight or flight, freeze, or any other involuntary physical response.

I want be very careful to distinguish between physical sensations and emotional feelings so you don't get confused. Physical sensations that are not an effect of thought are involuntary responses. These responses are typically caused by our "primitive brain" and evolved initially to keep us alive and safe from predator attacks, starvation and extinction. Our fight or flight response may be initiated in our body before any cognition has a chance to occur. For example, when a snake strikes out at you from behind a pane of glass at the zoo, your body may have a "flight" reaction that proceeds thought. This reaction is an involuntary primitive response patterned in the brain. When physical responses are involuntary, we do not note them in the feeling line of the model; in fact, they are circumstances due to the fact that we do not have direct control over them.

Hunger, illness, physical pain, and a "flight" response are all circumstances that may trigger thoughts. We can decide what to think and how to interpret these circumstances just like any other external circumstance. In the example of the snake striking out, the thought may be, "Don't worry, the snake is behind glass. You are safe." With this thought, there is the immediate dissipation of the flight response.

Every thought causes a feeling. The feeling is the effect of the thought. I must say this a thousand times a week. A client will tell me that they believe something and I will ask them if the thought is valid. Many times they will say, "It feels valid." That is of course how it feels—because you are thinking it.

An emotion is a vibration in your body. I like to think of the image of being injected with a pure feeling so we could just sit and watch ourselves experience it in our bodies without the thought causing it. I think this would make it easier to truly describe the feeling without the brain chatter in the way. I like to use words like tight, fast, shallow or hot to describe anxious feelings because that is how they generally feel in my body. I like to use words like slow, open, deep or expanding to describe peaceful feelings because that is how they feel to me.

Many times my clients will try to describe the feeling with another thought. I will say, "So how does that feel?" and they will say, "It feels like she shouldn't do that to me." Note that this is not the feeling but the thought causing the feeling. A feeling is a vibration in the body, not a sentence in the mind. Following is a long list of feelings that might help you when you are trying to identify what is going on when you connect to the vibration in your body. Try to think of feelings as single words and not as sentences, which are usually thoughts. When you look at a feeling on the list, try to imagine and describe what that feeling feels like. Are there many of these feelings that you have on a regular basis?

Being present with your feelings is like opening a conscious doorway to your thoughts. Our feelings are caused by our thoughts. Some are caused by patterns of thoughts or beliefs. A belief is a thought you keep on thinking or have been thinking for many years that causes you to feel the same feeling over and over.

The best way to understand yourself intimately is to feel your feelings from a place of consciousness. When you go through your day, ask yourself what you are feeling. Name the feeling and think about what it feels like in your body.

For example: FEAR

It is a fast vibration in my body. It vibrates very fast in my heart and chest. I notice my breath becomes shallow. I notice my eyes open wider. I notice the desire to move and take action. I hear a slight buzz in my ears. This is fear. I am in fear. I am doing fear. This is what fear feels like.

The more specific you can be in describing your emotions the better. Try to see yourself from a different perspective while you are in the emotion. Notice if you try to escape the emotion. Notice if you try to avoid it or detach from it. Notice how long the feeling lasts if you stay with it. Notice any resistance to it.

Sample Feelings List

❑ Happy ❑ Sad ❑ Angry ❑ Confused ❑ Elated ❑ Depressed
❑ Furious ❑ Bewildered ❑ Excited ❑ Disappointed ❑ Enraged
❑ Trapped ❑ Overjoyed ❑ Alone ❑ Outraged ❑ Troubled ❑ Thrilled
❑ Hurt ❑ Aggravated ❑ Desperate ❑ Exuberant ❑ Left Out ❑ Irate
❑ Lost ❑ Ecstatic ❑ Dejected ❑ Seething ❑ Fired Up ❑ Hopeless
❑ Delighted ❑ Sorrowful ❑ Crushed

MEDIUM

❑ Cheerful ❑ Heartbroken ❑ Upset ❑ Disorganized ❑ Up ❑ Down
❑ Mad ❑ Foggy ❑ Good ❑ Upset ❑ Annoyed ❑ Misplaced
❑ Relieved ❑ Distressed ❑ Frustrated ❑ Disoriented ❑ Satisfied
❑ Regretful ❑ Agitated ❑ Mixed Up ❑ Contented ❑ Hot
❑ Disgusted

MILD

❑ Glad ❑ Unhappy ❑ Perturbed ❑ Unsure ❑ Content ❑ Moody
❑ Uptight ❑ Puzzled ❑ Satisfied ❑ Blue ❑ Dismayed ❑ Bothered
❑ Pleasant ❑ Sorry ❑ Put-Out ❑ Uncomfortable ❑ Fine ❑ Lost
❑ Irritated ❑ Undecided ❑ Mellow ❑ Bad ❑ Touchy ❑ Baffled
❑ Pleased ❑ Dissatisfied ❑ Perplexed

❑ Afraid ❑ Weak ❑ Strong ❑ Guilty❑ Terrified ❑ Helpless
❑ Powerful ❑ Sorrowful ❑ Horrified ❑ Hopeless ❑ Aggressive
❑ Remorseful ❑ Scared Stiff ❑ Beat ❑ Gung Ho ❑ Ashamed
❑ Petrified ❑ Overwhelmed ❑ Potent ❑ Unworthy ❑ Fearful
❑ Impotent ❑ Super ❑ Worthless ❑ Panicky ❑ Small ❑ Forceful
❑ Exhausted ❑ Proud ❑ Drained ❑ Determined ❑ Scared
❑ Dependent ❑ Energetic ❑ Sorry ❑ Frightened ❑ Incapable
❑ Capable ❑ Lowdown ❑ Threatened ❑ Lifeless ❑ Confident
❑ Sneaky ❑ Insecure ❑ Tired ❑ Persuasive ❑ Uneasy
❑ Rundown ❑ Sure ❑ Shocked ❑ Lazy ❑ Insecure ❑ Shy
❑ Apprehensive ❑ Unsatisfied ❑ Secure ❑ Embarrassed
❑ Nervous ❑ Under Par ❑ Durable ❑ Worried ❑ Shaky ❑ Adequate
❑ Timid ❑ Unsure ❑ Able ❑ Unsure ❑ Soft ❑ Capable ❑ Anxious
❑ Lethargic ❑ Inadequate

One of the most common feelings my clients say they are feeling is stress and/or anxiety. I call these "cover emotions or feelings" (notice I use the word emotion and feeling interchangeably). Anxiety is usually the *fight against a feeling*. So, for example, maybe you are thinking a thought that your boss should have given you a raise when he didn't. This may cause a feeling of disappointment or anger. But because you don't want to feel this negative emotion or explore what is going on for you, you simply fight feeling it. You push it away and ignore it. As it comes back, you fight harder to keep it down and that fight feels like anxiety. I think many forms of depression are actually the exhaustion that follows this unwinnable fight.

One of the things I sometimes suggest my clients do is intentionally intensify the feeling. This is one way to break the pattern of action. So if you feel yourself getting anxious, you can try to intensify the anxiety. Increase the vibration. Really over-exaggerate the feeling. For clients who have been conditioned to fight emotion, this can be a huge step in getting more in touch with their bodies and more access to their thinking. By increasing the feeling, they are actually taking control of it and seeing that it is not something happening to them, but something they can increase and therefore decrease.

In my last book, I also had a chapter on feelings and one of my suggestions was to use the metaphor of a room for each feeling. Instead of pushing your back against the door of the room and trying to hold it closed and keep the feeling away, open the door. Walk in and look around the room. Notice everything about what is going on in your body when you are in this room of your emotion. This is a very different experience than trying to hold the bursting door closed and locking the emotion away in a dark, festering room of feelings. We aren't sure exactly what's in the room sometimes, and yet we are so busy fighting against it that we can't describe the feeling, let alone the thought causing it.

Can you see how this constant fighting and ignoring the genuine feeling can be a vicious cycle? It spins us away from getting access. If you are conscious enough to feel the emotion of disappointment all the way through, you can ask, "What is causing this feeling?" and find the thought. From here, you have the choice and power to change your thinking and relieve the feeling. You can end the ongoing battle not to feel.

As my clients begin this process, they often come back to me and say that they feel worse than before they started with me. I remind them that they don't feel worse, they are just more aware now. They have just become more conscious of how bad they really feel. This is a good thing. From this new consciousness, they can decide to change and not be at the mercy of unconscious thought and feeling.

Your feelings will always tell you clearly the nature of your thoughts. If you feel crappy all the time, it means you have crappy thoughts. If you feel happy all the time, you have happy thoughts. This is how it works. Knowing and remembering this truth will help you to not overlook many thoughts that may go unnoticed as being negative. Even when a thought appears to be positive, you must check it by asking yourself how the thought feels.

For example, about a year ago I had been working with a client for four months and felt like our coaching was completed. This client insisted I keep working with him, even though I state very clearly at the beginning of any coaching relationship that I do intense, short-term coaching. I struggled for hours with my own coach on how to speak my truth and let this client know I would not be keeping him on as a regular client. I wanted to let him know that he was ready to apply the work on his own and his dependence on me was unhelpful and possibly holding him back. I first tried practicing the thought, "I am done coaching him." Although true, this thought brought up the feeling of guilt within my body. When I changed the thought to, "Our time together is complete for now," I felt peaceful and relaxed. They are similar sounding thoughts, but they caused me completely different feelings and would have created very different results. I have found it nearly impossible to have a bad feeling thought lead to a permanent good result, so I always check my thoughts before I take action.

Yeah, but...what about the starving children in Africa? What about the abused children in America? What about the woman who has three mouths to feed and has no money? First, let me just say that I find it fascinating that many times when I propose that improving your life is as simple as changing your thinking, my clients seem to come up with some evidence that they are sure will shoot a hole in my theory. And usually the example is some outlandish circumstance that is in no way related to their life or reality. So before you let your left brain feed the belief, "It can't be this easy," I want you to sit with it for a minute, and allow yourself to notice the truth in it. You are not starving in Africa. You are not currently being beat over the head while reading. You are here reading this book. Does this truth apply to you? And if you think it doesn't, ask yourself why. Is that really a valid reason? My guess is not. I haven't had a client yet who has not seen the power of this work.

So as far as the people who have dire circumstances, the only thing of value I can say is that changing your thinking may not completely or immediately remove the physical pain of hunger or abuse or neglect, but it can make it better or worse. You can be a mom with no money or a starving child, and your thoughts about your circumstance will increase your suffering or decrease it. There is no doubt of that. If you are starving and you think thoughts of pain, your pain will be increased. If you are starving and you think thoughts of love, your feeling of love will be increased. This does not take away from the severity of physical pain and suffering but the truth is, the way you think about it does either add to or decrease your suffering. Even with ample justification for thinking negative thoughts, you are still just thinking negatively and creating more negative feelings.

My brother and I grew up in the same household. We had the same depressed mom and the same philandering, unavailable father. We shared many of the same circumstances, and yet his thoughts led him to unbearable feelings of pain that led him to the action of becoming addicted to drugs. He died of a cocaine overdose at the age of 30. My thoughts led me to a life filled with self-love, an amazing husband, and two beautiful children. I have a life filled with joy and love and happiness—no doubt because I had the ability and desire to take control of my own thinking. Same circumstances. Different thoughts.

Stop and take a deep breath.

How are you feeling right now?

That is also how you are thinking right now.

Look at the list of feelings again. Which of these feelings do you most want to have in this moment? What is the feeling you are seeking? You may think you are seeking money or a lover or a new apartment, but what you are really always seeking is a feeling that you believe that item or circumstance will create for you. Knowing now that your thoughts create your feelings, you may realize that you don't need to achieve these goals or have these things to feel good. You can change your thoughts and feel good now. This is the trick with the Law of Attraction—feel the feeling and experience the vibration *now* to attract the thing you want. You will then realize the thing you want will just be a cherry on top of the emotion you have been experiencing while you wait.

If you want the feeling of elation, all you need to do is to find the thought that would cause that feeling and think it. I swear. It really is that simple. Oh! I almost forgot. In order to get the feeling of the thought you are thinking you have to ***believe*** the thought you are thinking. Minor point. But the good news is that just like you can decide what to think and therefore feel, you can also decide what to believe.

This is where the Byron Katie work is so awesome. Any thought you believe that causes you pain, you can stop believing. The theory is simple according to Katie. Any thought that causes you pain is simply not true. Abraham would back her up on this. They would say any thought that causes you pain is a thought that is not aligned with your true self. Remember we are not arguing about circumstances being true here—just our thoughts about circumstances. So you can tell a thought needs to be questioned if it causes you pain.

If you want to feel passion—think a passionate thought. And how do you believe a passionate thought? You change the thought until you believe it and feel passion. For example, I can think the thought, "This Self Coaching 101 model will reduce the suffering of the world." Okay…I don't feel any passion. I don't believe that my little book will end world suffering. But I do believe using this model could end *some* of the needless suffering in the world. I believe this. I truly do, and when I think this thought I get so excited and passionate about writing, I take action and I actually write. Seriously. Did it today. Thought that thought, felt the passion it caused, and that is why you are reading these words.

This is the main difference between saying an affirmation and believing the affirmation. You can say the affirmation in hopes that someday you will believe it and feel good, or you can say an affirmation that you believe now and you will feel good now. Feeling good is contagious and will attract more feeling good thoughts and that will lead to feeling good actions which lead to good results.

Here are some examples of thoughts my clients created that they can believe to feel good:

- ✧ I can do me better than anyone in the world. (relief)
- ✧ I am here for a very important and exciting reason. (excitement)
- ✧ I have unlimited love to give. (love)
- ✧ It is cool being smart and good at math. (capable)
- ✧ My body is healthy and vibrant. (peaceful)
- ✧ I am able to thrive in this environment. (passionate)

Every drug we take for non-health reasons, every food we overeat, every cigarette we smoke or every porn flick we watch is to change how we feel. We try to treat the symptom. We try to change the feeling without locating its cause. We dull our emotional pain by covering it up. We put drugs and food and sex and overworking on top of our pain in hopes that we won't notice. But we do notice. The pain is there and when it goes unchecked, it gets bigger and shows up in our lives and in our bodies.

We cover it up, we fight it, we run from it, and we project it onto others. Anything but feel it! Why the heck is that? Why don't we just buzz with the vibration of feeling? Seriously, think about how much "war" would be prevented if we would just feel our feelings instead of reacting to them. Finding the cause and changing the cause of our feelings (our thoughts—not the terrorists' thoughts, by the way) so we feel better. Imagine that for a sec.

Feels good, right? That's because you're imagining a world based on conscious thoughtful thought and not impulsive reactivity. It's possible. It begins by being aware of what you are feeling. Self awareness and emotional intelligence begin with you, and they can literally change your experience of the world.

Think about this right now: What are your top three desired feelings? Write them down. Mine are peace, love, and excitement. What are the thoughts that you have to believe to be true to create these feelings in your body? My thought for peace is, "Everything happens exactly the way it is supposed to—perfectly." I do believe this, so when I think it I feel peaceful. I remind myself to think and feel peace often, especially when the circumstances seem to trigger alternate thoughts. My feeling of love is caused by my thought, "Everyone in my life is unbelievably amazing." My thought for excited is, "There's nothing I genuinely want that I can't have if I stay aligned."

Now it is your turn. Being aware of your negative thoughts and feelings is just the first step—now decide how you want to feel instead.

What are the top three feelings you want to feel? Write them here:

1. ______________________________
2. ______________________________
3. ______________________________

What are the respective thoughts you can think to feel these feelings?

1. ______________________________
2. ______________________________
3. ______________________________

I will finish up this chapter by giving you a very powerful example of this based on a client's experience.

Elizabeth was attending my retreat in Lake Tahoe which includes a rope course. She was on a ladder made of rope that extended many feet into the sky. Her primitive brain was in "flight" mode, causing her body to vibrate at a very high rate involuntarily. The brain was perceiving that she was in danger, and it triggered thoughts like: RUN, GET DOWN, STOP CLIMBING, YOU ARE IN DANGER. It was at this point that her involuntary reaction (the circumstance) triggered thoughts that she could choose to manage.

As I coached her, she began to allow herself to feel the feelings of fear with awareness and access the thoughts her involuntary response had triggered. I had her say them out loud to me, "I am scared of falling. I am going to get hurt. I can't do this. I am afraid of heights." I also had her consciously increase the feeling of fear in her body so the vibration felt less involuntary and more within her control. As the ladder shook due to the wind and her body movement, I had her move it more and shake it so she felt in control of the movement. Then, as she stayed focused as the Watcher, able to observe herself and describe her experience to me, she decided what she wanted to feel: calm and strong. I asked her what she would have to think in order to feel calm. She said, "I am safe. I am strong. I believe in myself. I can do this." She repeated the new thoughts out loud over and over as she climbed that ladder. This caused her to feel calm and confident, which led to the ultimate action of not only climbing the ladder, but letting go and belaying down, which had been unthinkable just minutes before.

She changed her thoughts and therefore her result. Ultimately this is how we change our lives.

FEELING PROBLEM WORKSHEET

What is the negative feeling? ______________________________

____

What is the thought causing this feeling? ______________________________

____

____

How do you act/react when you feel this way? ______________________________

____

____

What are the results of this action? ______________________________

____

____

How does this result prove the original thought? ______________________________

____

____

What would you like to be feeling? ______________________________

____

____

What thought could you think/believe that would cause this feeling?

____

____

Use the questions above to fill in the unintentional thought patterns.

UNINTENTIONAL THOUGHT PATTERN

CIRCUMSTANCE: ____________________

____

____

THOUGHT: ____________________

____

____

FEELING: ____________________

____

____

ACTION: ____________________

____

____

RESULT: ____________________

____

____

INTENTIONAL THOUGHT PATTERN

CIRCUMSTANCE: ____________________

____

____

NEW THOUGHT: ____________________

____

____

FEELING: ____________________

____

____

ACTION: ____________________

____

____

RESULT: ____________________

____

____

CHAPTER 5

Model in Detail:

ACTIONS

"What we do or not do."

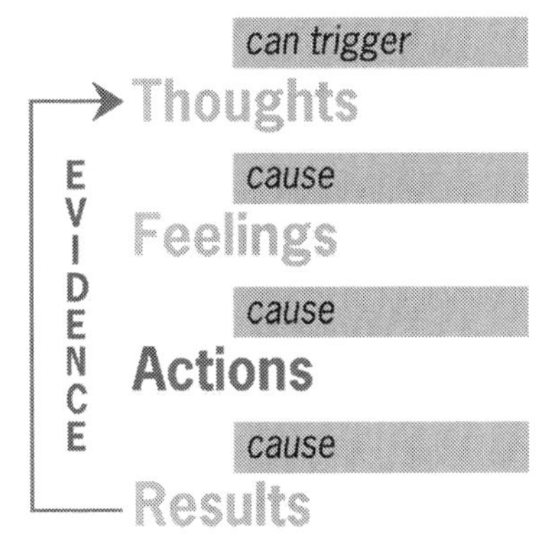

Finally! The doing! What can we DO about it? Take action. Get moving. Just do it. Get to work already! All this thinking and feeling and musing—when are we going to get to work and change the world?

Or maybe that is not you at all. Maybe you have your vision board and have been saying affirmations and wondering where your money and your success are. Either way, action may not be what you think it is. It's not just doing and doing and doing the same thing and wondering what heck is wrong. And it is not doing nothing and waiting for your ship to come in or for your knight in shining armor or for your winning lottery ticket.

Most coaching programs I've seen are all about the taking action piece and the getting the result piece, without consideration of the thought being the cause of the action. This type of work leads to a constant struggle of action against the unchanged thought. As shown in the attempt-to-change spin cycle diagram, eventually something has to give—it is either the original thought that changes, or the action stops, and therefore the result changes. **There is no amount of action that can make up for negative thinking.** The result either proves the original thought, or struggle occurs. In most cases, the thought never changes, and the result goes back to proving the original thought.

I cannot repeat this enough. If you want to change your behavior, you must change the thought first in order for the change to be permanent. Many of the changes we make in our lives naturally allow for this to happen without us noticing. When we decide we want to lose weight we may change our thinking to, "I can no longer live this way, I deserve better." Without even realizing it, the new thought has started a new thought-feeling-action-result cycle that motivates us to go to the gym and eat healthier food. Ultimately, we lose weight as a result. Other times we may have attempted to go to the gym and eat healthy but we kept thinking the old thought: I don't deserve a thinner body, I am lazy, this is what I was dealt. In this case, our effort (action) will ultimately change back to support the thought we are thinking.

Common actions people want to change are eating, spending, drinking, working, worrying, gossiping and procrastinating, just to name a few. When we notice these behaviors (actions) and their results in our lives, we commonly fall into the trap of self-sabotage by thinking even more negative thoughts. If we are yelling at our kids because we feel worry from the thought "My kids don't behave," we sometimes end up worrying about the yelling and the effect of the yelling creates new thoughts (I am a terrible mother, for example) that leads to even more worry, stress, and yelling.

The first step is in asking, "Why do you do what you do? What are the thoughts and feelings that drive your behavior?" You can then ask what it is you want to do. When you know the behavior you are seeking to practice, you can ask, "What thought do I need to think?" in order to lead to that behavior. By thinking the new thought and believing it, you drive new action, which leads to new results, which provide evidence for the new thought.

Taking "aligned" and thoughtful action based on newly created thought helps us transcend our circumstances even when they are not ideal. Tony likes to call it "massive action." Eckhart calls it "awakened doing." Whatever you want to call it is fine with me. After you change your thinking, you make the change permanent with supporting action.

Action can provide evidence for our new thoughts. When we take action, we are either proving or disproving our thoughts by the results we are creating. As we take action, we are chipping away at old thoughts and breaking up long established patterns of action.

For example, if you are an overspending kind of thinker, and you think thoughts like "Buying stuff feels good," you are going to feel compulsive and anxious until you take action and buy the shoes on sale at Nordstrom. The result will be that credit card bill that you are afraid to open, let alone pay. The result will prove that you need to do things to make yourself feel better—hey, what about shopping?

When you change your thought to "I don't need to shop to feel good," in the beginning you are going to need to take action to prove this true. You do this by NOT SHOPPING and thinking thoughts that feel good. At first this might seem difficult. And here is why: you have established a very familiar pattern of action caused by a very familiar pattern of thought and feeling. As you start to take action that deviates from this pattern, you might feel a bit out of place or "off." Plan on it. You brain has just been flipped out of autopilot and it can be very discombobulating. Also, that belief that you have held so close and dear—remember the one where shopping is the ultimate high? Well, let's just say it is going to be upset when you stop giving it evidence to stand on. It is like a hungry, chubby sentence that wants to be fed lots of proof. When you start disproving it, you now have a conflict with a deeply seated thought that is stored in your brain, with lots of emotion and evidence waiting to be activated by the next store. When you do the opposite and interrupt the pattern, the neurons supporting the belief literally weaken and stop firing. This is not good news for the little impulse that has been having quite a party in that small peanut-sized space in your brain.

Treat it like a small child having a tantrum. It's noisy—it may cause a fuss and some added vibration as it pulls out all its supporting thoughts and tries to make you believe them. Don't take the bait. Just notice. Don't buy. Forge a new pattern. Before you know it, you won't be able to remember why you ever thought buying a pair of shoes now was worth feeling awful later. Action that disproves a thought is how you manage Peanut and change your thinking forever.

Another thing to consider when looking at your life and the actions you want to take to get the results you want is how just one little step out of the old pattern changes everything. If you really wish you would exercise each morning, you must focus on the very first step that will change the pattern. It is not lifting the first weight at the gym that breaks this pattern—it is the moment you wake up earlier than normal, put your gym clothes on and grab the bottle of water. If you do only this, you have changed a pattern of action.

With my weight loss clients, I have them exercise for five minutes three times a week if they have been sedentary for many months. This five minutes won't change their calorie burn much, but it will change the pattern of thought-feeling-action. It will slowly chip away at a thought that says, "I don't work out," or "I am lazy." This small action is what can eventually change an entire identity.

Martha talks about doing turtle steps by taking one small action at a time. With me, for example, I kept thinking the thought, "I will never write another book because I hate writing." This thought led to a feeling of resistance. The action was *in*action: not writing. The result was no book. When I decided to change the thought to "I am going to write a book titled Self-Coaching 101 and it is going to help as many people as my first book," I felt excited. From this place of excitement, I did not write. I was nowhere near ready to write. I was in between thoughts at this point, needing to break my old, "I will never write again" pattern. So I emailed my book designer and had her design the cover. This was a very tiny action for me—literally just one email. But as soon as I saw that cover with my name on it, I knew that it would someday be a book. It was great evidence against my old thought and for my new one.

What action do you need to take to disprove your old, painful thought just a little? Think about this right now. What is the new thought? What feeling does it cause? What action can you take to build evidence for it now?

Following are some real client examples of the model at work. The first models show an undesired action put through the model and the rest show samples of how to use the model to add a desired action or behavior.

Undesired Actions

C N/A
T I am too fat
F Anxious
A Overeating
R Gain Weight

C N/A
T I have nothing to say
F Uninspired
A Not writing my book
R Empty pages

C N/A
T He is shut down and not connecting
F Frustrated
A Yelling at my spouse
R He shuts down

C
T I'm not a good consultant
F Apathetic
A Not marketing my business
R No one hires me

Desired Actions

C N/A
T I love and am in control of my body
F Calm, peaceful, connected
A Eat healthy
R Energized, at my natural weight

C N/A
T My family is gonna love the new albums
F Motivated, inspired

A Work on albums regularly until complete
R Albums finished

C
T My thoughts determine my in-flow of money, not my action
F Confident, abundant
A Pay off mortgage
R No payments to bank

C
T If I run with my son every day. I can teach him the mental discipline to compete
F Excited, motivated, competitive
A Run in the morning with my son
R Time with son, time teaching my son, doing my best to help him

An important heads-up needs to go out to you as you begin to get inspired to take more action. As your thoughts change from negative to positive, you will notice an increase in your mental energy. The juicier and more exciting your thoughts, the more driven and energetic your action will be. But as you change these thoughts and feelings, you will literally be changing your self-concept and your identity in many ways. The new thoughts you think may be thoughts you've never thought before, which will lead to actions you have never taken or sustained before. As with anything new, you might feel worse before you feel better. You need to allow this and allow yourself to "suck at it" for a while. Never use action inspired by new thought as a reason to think new negative thoughts or to beat yourself up. With enough practice, the new action will cement your belief in the thought. It really is true when they say, stay with the new thought long enough to practice and cement the inspired action.

Finally, in closing out the chapter I want to emphasize that the main point of this book is that we must change our thoughts to change our lives. This is the same message you can read about in *The Secret* or any of the Law of Attraction materials. Thoughts are things and we create what we think about. But there is one big **but** that was underemphasized in *The Secret* and that is ACTION IS STILL REQUIRED. You cannot sit in your room staring at the wall and "attract" a toned body. You must change your thoughts first, and then you take the newly inspired action and keep thinking the new thought over and over until the pattern is changed permanently and becomes more effortless. Sorry, *The Secret* isn't a magic pill—it requires you to change your thought first and then take the action that new thought inspires.

ACTION PROBLEM WORKSHEET

What is the behavior you want to change? ____________________

____

____

____

What feelings do you experience prior to and during this behavior? __

____

____

____

____

What thoughts lead to this feeling and this behavior? (Answer anything here but "I don't know." Guess if you aren't sure.)________

____

____

What result do you get when you act this way?________________

____

____

How does this result prove the original thought that leads to this behavior? ____

____

What feelings might negate this behavior? ___________________

____

____

What thought would you need to think to feel this way? __________

____

____

____

Use the questions above to fill in the unintentional thought patterns.

UNINTENTIONAL THOUGHT PATTERN

CIRCUMSTANCE: ____

____

____

THOUGHT: ____

____

____

FEELING: ____

____

____

ACTION: ____

____

____

RESULT: ____

____

____

INTENTIONAL THOUGHT PATTERN

CIRCUMSTANCE: ____

____

____

NEW THOUGHT: ____

____

____

FEELING: ____

____

____

ACTION: ____

____

____

RESULT: ____

____

____

Notes:

CHAPTER 6

Model in Detail:

RESULTS

"The effect of action."

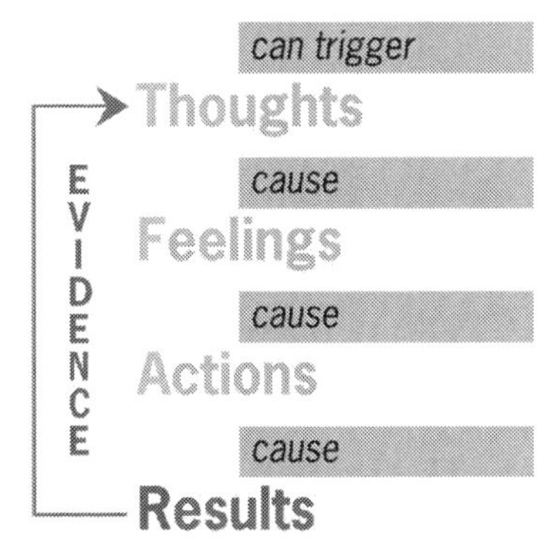

Do you know what you want? Really? What? How specific are you? Do you have a vision board covered with the results you want—your results, the ones you are going to create with your thoughts, feelings and actions? I am always so surprised when I ask people what they want and they say, "I don't know." They say they will just see what happens and take what comes, as if they aren't the ones who create it with their unconscious thinking. A life of reaction is more the norm than the exception. So take a few minutes right now and write a few sentences about the result you want in the following areas:

Family Relationships ______________________

____

____

____

Friendships ______________________

____

____

____

Work ______________________

____

____

____

Family Life ______________________

____

____

____

Home Life ______________________

____

____

____

Money ______________________

____

____

____

Spirituality ______________________________

____

____

____

10 years from now ______________________________

____

____

____

____

____

50 years from now ______________________________

____

____

____

____

____

How do your current results match up? Can you identify why you have or don't yet have the results you want? Can you pinpoint the exact thought? Can you distinguish the difference between your circumstances and your results?

In order to get what you want, you must think thoughts and believe thoughts that lead to the result. Negative thoughts do not lead to positive, long term results. They may give you temporary quick fixes, but they won't lead to long term satisfaction or to freedom from the struggle against negativity.

Pick one of the items from the list of things you want and fill out the LOA (Law of Attraction) worksheet.

LOA WORKSHEET

What do you want to have? (Pick one thing per worksheet)________

____

____

Why do you want to have this? What is the feeling you are seeking? _

____

____

What action would you take to have this result? Be specific. _______

____

____

What would you have to believe/think to get this result? ___________

____

____

When you believe/think this thought do you feel the way you want to feel? ____

____

____

Can you feel right now the way you want to feel when you get what you want? Why or why not?______________________________________

____

____

Do you have a current thought preventing this result? What is it?____

____

____

What is the new thought that will get you what you want?__________

____

____

Once you have completed the worksheet, plug your new thought into the model below:

Thought: ______________________________
Feeling: ______________________________
Action: ______________________________
Result: ______________________________

After you have the new thought, you will want to study the model with this new thought often. Feel the feeling of the thought, take the action of the feeling, and visualize the result as often as possible—the more the better. If "anti-thoughts" come up that try to counter your thought, plug them into another model and change them as many times as needed to create a new, better feeling thought/result pattern.

Now that you have used the model to attract what you want, what can you do if you are getting a result you don't want? By now you know the drill, but I will repeat it anyway. Tony always says that repetition is the mother of skill. The goal is to find the thought causing the unwanted result. You just need to get hold of one of these thoughts to break the pattern. You can get access to the thought by acknowledging the action leading to the result. Make sure you find your action—not the action of others. Others' actions are always circumstances. Then see if you can locate the feeling and thoughts that led to the action. Fill in the worksheet.

Now, to break this pattern, you need to change the thought. Find a better feeling thought that you believe. This can be challenging when the thought at first glance seems to be positive. A positive thought does not lead to a negative result, so check specifically how the thought feels. Sometimes when we are thinking about wanting something, we are actually feeling the lack of it. You may need to change even a positive sounding thought of want until it actually leads to a positive feeling of having it—and not the lack of it.

As you think this thought, notice the increase in positive feeling. Then take action to prove this thought. You are providing evidence against the original belief by taking new action (not by just thinking up evidence that it is not true.) You are actually "doing" evidence against it. More importantly, you are creating a new pattern by thinking a new thought, feeling a better feeling and taking a different action.

Let's go back to one of the previous examples. The thought was: My boss doesn't like me because I threaten him. Let's find a better feeling thought. Here's one example: I am likable and I want to show up in a way that I can feel proud of. So let's plug this one in.

Thought: I am likable and I want to show up in a way that I can feel proud of.
Feeling: Encouraged
Action: Contribute in meetings when I genuinely feel I have something to offer the team.
Result: People will know more about me and my work.

This is a very likely result. Although there is no way to know what the result ultimately will be, playing out this model can break very old patterns by just taking new actions. When you think about the results you want in your life, you can work the model backwards to get to the thought work that is necessary.

If the result you want is stated as "I want to have one million dollars," then I can ask myself the following questions:

What type of action will I take to make/manifest one million dollars?
What feelings would most help me take this action?
What thoughts do I want to believe/think in order to create this feeling?

New Thoughts
I am capable of increasing my income significantly with this new job.
I know many people who are millionaires and if they can do it, so can I.

Feelings
Capable
Excited
Passionate

Actions
Pass out business cards.
Hire a publicist.
Create a new website.
Write a book.
Hire a financial coach.
Run my financial statements.
Get on a budget.
Start doing more appearances to get clients.

Result
Plan in place to be millionaire within three years following current budget and income plans.

It truly is this simple:

Name the problem or issue, whether it is a thought, feeling, action or result in your life.
Fill in the model.
Change the thought to one that will give you the feeling/action/result you want. (It must be a thought you genuinely believe.)
Take action to provide evidence for the new thought/belief.

Here is how I lost weight with this model:

Brooke overweight
Thought: I will always have a weight issue.
Feeling: Defeated
Action: Did not exercise and ate compulsively.
Result: Gained weight or maintained overweight.

Brooke at natural weight
Thought: My body is wise and without me interfering has no problems.
Feeling: trusting, relaxed, self-love, hopeful
Action: Exercised, ate when my body told me to and stopped when it told me to.
Result: Lost 70 pounds and have maintained it for 6 years.

The other piece to this, which I did not teach in the original class, is that sometimes the result is an additional thought. That's right. So you have a thought that leads to another thought that leads to another thought. Before you know it, you have a pattern of thought and action that creates a result of a system of negative thinking and feeling. It looks something like this:

Thought
Feeling
Action
Result Thought
    Feeling
    Action
    Result Thought
        Feeling
        Action
        Result

Thought: My boss doesn't like me because I threaten him.
Feeling: Insecure
Action: Act quiet and reserved in meetings.
Result Thought: Nobody cares what I have to say because I am threatening.
    Feeling: Insignificant
    Action: Avoid talking to coworkers.
    Result: Thought: I have no friends because I threaten them.
        Feeling: sad
        Action: Don't go out or attend social functions.
        Result: Isolation

Isolation feeds back into the three thoughts: "I have no friends," "Nobody cares what I have to say," and "My boss doesn't like me." This is a classic belief system. It feeds on other thoughts, actions, and feelings.

When you have patterns of thoughts that you keep thinking, I call it a belief system. A collection of belief systems is ultimately what makes you—you. It's your identity. Thoughts build on thoughts and provide evidence for each other. When you have a healthy, positive belief system, this is great news. When you have a negative belief system and you are getting consistently negative results in your life, it will take some thought unraveling to change to a better identity. That being said, remember that "overwhelmed" is just another feeling caused by a thought and does not need to derail your efforts. Just take one thought at a time, even when the thought is a result of another thought, and keep unwinding until you feel the relief of the better feeling. Remember the distinction, I previously mentioned, between a result and a circumstance. A result is something you have created in your life with your thinking. It can include manifestations from the Law of Attraction, but for the point of this model I differentiate between circumstances that we don't have direct control over and our results, which we do have direct control over.

Here are some examples:

Not having any friends (result)
A friend moving out of state (circumstance)
Having a job you hate (result)
Your company going out of business (circumstance)
Having a combative relationship with your son (result)
Having a son with behavioral issues (circumstance)

I don't want you to get too caught up in monitoring and managing your results. Sometimes the results you create now become circumstances you can't immediately control later (obesity being an example of this).

But it is important to understand that the results in this model always prove the original thought that led to the feeling/action/result pattern.

RESULT PROBLEM WORKSHEET

What is a negative result you currently have in your life? ____________

____

____

What action leads to this result? ____________________________

____

____

What feelings cause this action? ____________________________

____

____

What thoughts cause this feeling? ___________________________

____

____

What is the opposite of this current thought? __________________

____

____

What result would the opposite thought create? ______________

____

____

What is the result you want to have? _________________________

____

____

What is the thought you can think and believe to achieve this result?

____

____

____

Use the questions above to fill in the unintentional thought patterns.

UNINTENTIONAL THOUGHT PATTERN

CIRCUMSTANCE: ______________________________

____

____

THOUGHT: ______________________________

____

____

FEELING: ______________________________

____

____

ACTION: ______________________________

____

____

RESULT: ______________________________

____

____

INTENTIONAL THOUGHT PATTERN

CIRCUMSTANCE: ______________________________

____

____

NEW THOUGHT: ______________________________

____

____

FEELING: ______________________________

____

____

ACTION: ______________________________

____

____

RESULT: ______________________________

____

____

LOA WORKSHEET

What do you want to have? (Pick one thing per worksheet)________

____

Why do you want to have this? What is the feeling you are seeking?

____

What action would you take to have this result? Be specific. _______

____

What would you have to believe/think to get this result? ___________

____

____

When you believe/think this thought do you feel the way you want to feel? ____

Can you feel right now the way you want to feel when you get what you want? Why or why not?_________________________________

____

____

Do you have a current thought preventing this result? What is it?____

____

____

What is the new thought that will get you what you want?__________

____

____

Once you have completed the worksheet, plug your new thought into the model below:

Thought: ____________________________________

Feeling: ____________________________________

Action: _____________________________________

Result: _____________________________________

CHAPTER 7

Common Questions

What if I can't figure out what I am feeling?
Breathe. Sit still. Ask yourself if you feel more mad, glad, sad, or happy. This is more an art than a science. You don't have to be too specific for this to work. If you feel negatively, it is worth doing the work to find the thought causing it. The more you get in touch with your body and the different vibrational frequencies that different thoughts cause, the more you will be able to identify and name your feelings more specifically.

Does thought always cause my feelings? Isn't it sometimes the feelings causing my thinking? Can a feeling just "come over" me?
There are two ways we experience a feeling. One way is through physical sensations caused by involuntary physical response and the other way is by our thinking. There are times when our feelings are a physical response that precedes our thought. In the example of being on a roller coaster, you may feel fear based on the stimuli of the height of the cart and the sensation of the movement—this feeling is a physical reaction that

moves straight from the senses to the amygdala and then through the body without passing through the brain. But just seconds later we process the stimuli through the brain and think a thought that either intensifies the fear (I am going to die!) or lessens the fear (This is just a ride and I am going to be fine. This is fun.)

For the sake of this work the most important distinction is in understanding that our thoughts—not our circumstances or other people—cause our feelings. Even with involuntary physical reactions, the feeling and vibration is intensified or lessened by our thought.

Do we always want to change our feelings? Should we try to never feel a negative feeling?
I believe some feelings that appear to be negative are completely appropriate. Grief, exhaustion, and pain are feelings I willingly feel on occasion. The thoughts that cause these emotions seem appropriate to me sometimes and feeling these feelings all the way through is cleansing to me. I am careful not to get stuck in the spin cycle of feeling negatively, but I do allow a cycle of feeling when it feels clean and human to do so.

How do I work this model when I am at work or surrounded by people?
It is kind of like practicing for a game. The more you practice this at home alone, the better you will get at doing it real-time when you are with people. In the beginning you may need to do the model work after the circumstance, but as you get better you can redirect yourself during a circumstance. (That's when it really gets fun.)

Is it important to always write it down?
In the beginning I recommend you write it down using a worksheet and get the thoughts on paper. I have many scraps of paper and napkins that I start by writing this on:

C
T
F
A
R

This can be done anywhere and gets the thought out of my head so I can see it more clearly. Once you get better at it you might be able to do it quickly in your head, but for painful thoughts I still write out and complete the entire model.

Do I have to fill out the model with the new thought? Can't I just change the thought?
The whole goal is to change the thought and if it works for you to just create a new thought and believe it, then by all means do that. Most of us need to see the full effect of the thought and understand it deeply before we can create a whole new way of thinking. This model is a great tool for doing that quickly.

You say that it is my thought causing the feelings, but what if it really is just my husband? He really does say negative things to me—I don't just "think" he does.
It is never the husband. You can't outsource your feelings. His actions are caused by *his* feelings and his thoughts cause *his* feelings, not yours. I believe that your husband says negative things to you, but I don't believe

that what your husband says causes your feelings. What you think about what your husband says is what causes your feelings. If you believe him or think he is disrespecting you or if you think he should be behaving in a way that is different from reality, you will feel pain. No one causes your feelings but you. I know it is hard to break the habit of thinking, "He hurt my feelings," but that thought is always a lie. You hurt your feelings each and every time.

Now, again, I am not condoning his behavior or telling you to stay with a man who acts this way. I am just telling you the truth: that you are the one who makes the choices of who you are going to spend your time with, listen to, and believe. If you choose him and you believe him, you hurt your feelings.

Your model is very similar to another process I have used before—can I use both?
Of course! You can and should use anything that works for you. I have heard from many people that this model is very similar to other programs and processes and I am not surprised, because this really does work! Take from all your favorite teachers and tools and use the mixture that helps you best create the life you want.

How is the new thought different from just an affirmation?
It's not. An affirmation is really just an affirming thought. The main difference in the way it is presented here is that I don't recommend you use an affirmation that you don't believe. I do not believe in saying things that you aren't believing over and over again until you believe them. This has never worked for me. When I

was heavier I could say, "You are so skinny" all day long in my head but it was always accompanied by the thought "No, you're not," and so it caused a feeling of inadequacy and not peace.

Can it really be this simple? I am afraid this feeling of relief won't last.
Take that thought and plug it into the model. If you believe it won't last, you will end up taking action to prove it true.

It is this simple? Yes. Easy? Not always. The feeling of relief is always just one thought away.

What if I don't think my result proves my original thought?
Then you don't have the correct thought for the result. The result will always prove the original thought. This is a common beginner's mistake. Sometimes we have so many thoughts at once it is hard to find and pinpoint the thought creating the result. With practice you will be able to identify the thought and its result as evidence for it quite easily.

Can two different thoughts cause the same feeling? All my thoughts seem to cause me to feel hopeless all the time.
Yes. Many thoughts can cause the feeling of hopelessness or any other emotion. These thoughts will keep strengthening their own spin cycle and create evidence for each other. This is a negative belief system that is a web of negative thinking and feelings. Unravel each thought one at a time. As you continue to work through your negative beliefs, many of the supporting thoughts will simply fall away.

Can't we take action and change our results without changing our thoughts? Can we move up the model backward?
Yes. This can work and I have seen it work, but this is definitely the hard way. It is much easier to change the thought and then take action to prove it true than to take action against a negative thought. But yes, it can be done. Just make sure you have truly changed the thought or your new results will be temporary.

I want my wife to use this model but she won't. I can't do this alone.
You can totally do this alone. You can't control your wife or her behavior, even though many of us do try. I have found the best way to inspire people to do this thought work is to show your life as an example. The results will speak for themselves.

Are excuses the same as thoughts?
Yes. Plug any excuse into the model and you will see the result it gets you.

I find it hard to admit some of the thoughts I am thinking. How can I get over this?
Ask yourself why it is hard to admit your painful thoughts. This answer is a great thought to start with. Remember, you don't have to admit these thoughts to anyone but yourself. Also, one of the reasons some of us have a hard time admitting our thoughts is that we beat ourselves up for our thinking. This serves no purpose and has no upside. Try to be curious and kind when doing this work. Be a compassionate student of yourself. Know that there is a reason why you think the way you do and it is okay. It is also okay to change your thoughts now.

What if I want to feel a negative emotion?
Sometimes you will, and sometimes it is completely appropriate to fully feel emotions commonly termed negative such as grief, sadness, loss, loneliness, disappointment and fear. I would never suggest you try to change your thoughts if you are not suffering. Feeling emotions cleanly through is not suffering. The key with any emotion is to feel it with awareness and notice the thoughts causing you to feel deeply. Typically, genuinely felt emotion—even "negative" emotion—passes naturally and gently when it is not caused by an untrue thought. An example of this might be "I miss my dog Calvin who passed away." This is a genuine and what I would call a clean thought that may cause clean negative emotion. This is not the same as a suffering thought that might be "If only I had paid better attention, he would not have drowned in the pool." This also causes negative emotion, but it is riddled with pain and guilt caused by an argument with reality and the past.

I am having a hard time with this. Can you coach me using this model?
I can and do coach many clients and I teach coaches how to coach using this method. But before you hire one of us, take your time and be willing to suck at this long enough to get good at it. In the beginning you may struggle a bit with getting it on paper, but as you continue, my guess is that you will notice a huge shift in the way you see yourself and your own thinking. I get many e-mails per week from my students who are excited that they finally "got it" and now use the model daily in their lives with very little struggle.

FORUM DISCUSSION SAMPLES

These have been lightly edited for easier reading and to preserve privacy.

Example one:

CLIENT: *Hi Brooke, I haven't heard your audio class yet but I've read your PDF materials.*

I apologize for the following long question, but this is an issue that continues to wreak havoc on my body and my mind.

My question is, with regards to my personal problem I seem to be able to identify my thoughts and I'm trying to do the turnarounds. But I'm frustrated that I am not seeing the results and actions that would best reflect a healthier relationship with myself. I have to write a dissertation and am finding a deadening dull feeling every time I sit down to write, despite having an outline and notes on what I want to say. I want the deadening feeling to go away. I want to be moved by the passion I have inside for the issues I'm engaging. Now at least I know that the deadened feeling is tied to a thought. I think the thought is that there is a "good" academic way to write and I shouldn't do it badly. There is not one way to do good academic work. These turnarounds feel good and I'm motivated, but then I sit down and the deadening dull feelings are still around. I've started to think I'm just lazy or I'm not supposed to do this work. But I know that the issues are important to me and I feel strongly about the field.

Do you have suggestions on how best to coach myself?

BROOKE: Hi! Great question. Before I answer, I have to say I don't remember anyone ever telling me that they felt passionate and excited writing a dissertation. I believe this is the reason that many people don't actually complete them.

Here is my suggestion. Don't fight the feeling of dread. When you go to start writing, plan on dread being your companion for a while. Get to know the texture of it. Have it be your writing buddy. I can feel you are fighting the dread and, dare I say, dreading the dread. This will only add to the trouble you have writing.

You may not be able to do this for long periods of time, but maybe just plan on writing for 30 minutes (with your new buddy Dread) each day. I think you might be surprised what happens if you do this.

It has worked beautifully for me in many things I have wanted to have done but didn't want to do.

By not dreading the dread you are removing one layer of negativity. That is a great place to start.

CLIENT: *I love it. Thanks Brooke. You have a way of understanding that is incisive and cuts through to me. I absolutely dread the dread. I pine away. Ok, I'm going to give this new exercise a try!*

Example two:

CLIENT: *Hi Brooke! I absolutely love your work. I have your Coach in a Box set and have also listened to your Self Coaching 101 class. I am really doing the work! My issue is that I am overly concerned with what people think of me, especially at work. My coworkers are not my "tribe," so to speak—they are very conservative and have different lifestyles than I do. I find that I am extremely uncomfortable many times at work and worry about every little thing that I say. It definitely adds to my anxiety level, which in turn drives me to overeating/overdrinking.*

Do you have any suggestions for me on how to break out of this negative thinking pattern? I would just like to care less about what they think and care more about what I think.

Thank you again for your awesome teaching!

BROOKE: OK. So first let's play out the worst case scenario. What if everyone at work thinks you are horrible (in whatever way that would worry you the most)—what would that mean to you?

Also, when you watch what you are saying at work, are you trying to convince yourself that you can control what they think of you by what you say? Is there any part of you that thinks you can control them? How does it feel to try and control them?

CLIENT: *Hi Brooke. Thanks for your reply. Here are my answers.*

"What if everyone at work thinks you are horrible (in whatever way that would worry you the most) what would that mean to you?"

It would mean that I wasn't good enough somehow, that my suspicions are confirmed—that I don't measure up. Okay, that uncovered a pretty powerful belief right there. WOW.

"Also, when you watch what you are saying at work, are you trying to convince yourself that you can control

what they think of you by what you say? Is there any part of you that thinks you can control them? How does it feel to try and control them?"

And the answer to the first question is absolutely YES. I think I can control what they think of me by watching every little word I say. I guess I must think I can control them, which is an illusion. I can't control them. I can't control anyone. I want to be able to control them because I am afraid of not being liked. I'm afraid of confirming my beliefs that I am not good enough. So I obsessively watch what I say and beg them to like me in some not-so-subtle ways in order to stay "safe." I don't know if that makes any sense at all.

But it does feel like I'm fighting a losing battle. I think now I have to find a new belief, one that says I am good enough no matter if people like me or not. I've lived with the old one for a very long time.

BROOKE: If everyone thinks you're horrible it does not mean that you aren't good enough. It means that they think you are horrible. It tells us about them—not you.

If you act in a certain way so they will like you—they don't even like YOU—they like who you are pretending to be.

If you think you aren't good enough, you will look for evidence to prove your belief and you will find it. If you believe you are good enough, you don't need any evidence. People look to you to see how to treat you. How do you treat yourself?

When people beg me to like them I tend to like them less. I can't like them enough to make up for them not liking themselves.

Being liked is an inside job. Being enough is already done...you just haven't noticed.

You are good enough. Period.

Example three:

CLIENT: *Hi Brooke, Thank you for this class. It was excellent and right to the point. Okay— have a few questions:*

Q1: If the only moment we have is "NOW," why do we use "laws of attraction" to wish for things in the future? For example, "I will be a millionaire when I am 50 years old." Is it contradictory?

Q2. Once we have stated our desire to the universe, should we think about it every day to reinforce the feeling of "already having it," or just let go of it (as mentioned in Martha Beck's "love list") and let the Universe work for us?

Q3. I was asking my 60-year-old mother what she wants to change in her life. She said that she would like to be able to make more money because now she's economically dependent on her children. Should I tell her that she can manifest the wealth if she believes it? Or I should challenge her belief that she needs more money?

Q4. Do we have to feel abundant first to attract what we want in our life? What about many debt-ridden people who have spent money at will and never felt that money is scarce until they cannot pay their mortgage?

Reading your discussions with a previous client reminds me of a story a friend told me. She works in an advertising agency leading a team on the creative side. One colleague is obviously not up to the challenge of his tasks. His designs never convey the message the clients want and everybody in their team was unhappy about his performance. However this colleague is a very happy person. He has probably never doubted that that he is "good enough" and never realized that his designs were not meeting the expectations of the clients.

My question is, if we totally ignore what people think about us and just "feel good" about ourselves, do we lose contact with reality sometimes, just like this design guy? And how should my friend communicate with this colleague if he cannot believe that his work is not "good enough" for the clients?

Thank you!

BROOKE: Great questions. See my answers below:

1. The only moment we have is now and the reason we use law of attraction is to ALIGN our thinking in this moment in order to attract the reality we want. How we think and feel now is what determines what we have in the future. We must feel as if we have it now in order to create it in our lives. So even though it feels like we are "in the future," the law of attraction is really about how we feel in this moment NOW. The feeling is what brings the attraction and manifestation.

2. You can think about what you want and then let it go IF YOU REALLY BELIEVE IT IS COMING. You will know you can let it go because it FEELS GOOD TO KNOW THAT YOU DON'T EVER HAVE TO WORRY ABOUT GETTING IT. You already feel as though you have it, so when it actually manifests it is just a bonus. BUT—if you notice that

you still have some doubt that you will get it, you can do the thought work daily in order to align with the feeling that will ultimately attract it.

3. I suggest you challenge her belief and then tell her she can have it if she wants it and if she truly believes she needs it.

4. Debt-ridden people are not abundant. They spend more than they have in order to fill some void birthed out of scarcity. Going into debt unconsciously is not the same as living from a place of connected abundance.

Awesome questions!

Part 2 in response to the happy guy at work...

Good example to consider.

Knowing we are good enough does not mean we are not aware of our work or not open to feedback. In fact, just the opposite is true. People who have a deep sense of themselves can be very aware and open to feedback, because they do not confuse negative work/project feedback with their own sense of worth.

You don't have to totally ignore what other people think about you but using their opinion of you (not your work) as a reason to think you are not good enough is seeking evidence for a lie that serves no one.

Confusing quality work with the quality of a person is not what I meant to suggest in my conversation with the previous client at all. Two very different things.

Does that make sense to you? Would love to hear your thoughts.

CLIENT: *Hi Brooke,*

Thank you very much for your answers. They are

super brilliant and clear!! I have a few more questions if you don't mind:

1. If everything is acceptable, does that lead us to be indifferent? I understand that it helps to make me feel good, no matter what others are doing. However, if I tell myself that when somebody lies it is OK because I should not have a limiting belief that "people should not lie," and people do lie, does that mean that we should have very low expectations for people? I am wondering if I will go numb to the injustice I see in society because "people do it anyway."

I'm also wondering to what extent one should express expectations for others—e.g., your spouse—if all we can change is ourselves. What role should communications play here?

2. If nothing happens without our thoughts attracting it, what about those people who lost their valuable assets/possessions because of the fraudulent behavior of their close friends or family members? They probably have never imagined this happening; therefore they have not taken any precautions to prevent it. How do we explain "laws of attraction" in this case?

3. How do we relate "I" & "Ego" to "conscious and subconscious mind??" I know these are different sets of references but am interested to know if we can relate them in any way. I read that "conscious mind chooses what we want, and the subconscious mind takes that choice and creates the blueprint." Do you agree?

Thanks again, Brooke!

BROOKE:

1. My experience has been the complete opposite. Accepting reality is the first step to genuine change.

When someone lies to me and I can accept it, I am in a clear place to create a well-thought consequence (for my kids, for example) or make a decision (to take action in society).

You can express your expectations as much as you want, as long as you don't expect people to change to meet them.

2. The tricky thing to understand about law of attraction is that you don't necessarily have to think the EXACT thing that happens to you. People don't have to think "My family will commit fraud and I will lose my assets." They may just have a belief: "There will never be enough." This deep-seated belief can attract loss in many different forms.

3. They are very different references but you can use them in understanding that we have thoughts we are conscious of and thoughts that we are unconscious of. The process of becoming conscious of the thoughts that drive your action is the work.

CLIENT: *Hi Brooke! Thank you for your great answers! However I am not fully clear about "to create a well-thought consequence (for my kids, for example) or make a decision (to take action in society)." Would you please elaborate on that a little bit? Thank you.*

BROOKE: Yes. Here is what I mean.

Option 1:
My kid lies to me.
I have a thought, "My kid should not lie and he doesn't respect me."
I get angry because I think this thought.

I yell at my kid and tell him that he is grounded and can't play videos for a week.
I fume for hours and give him the silent treatment.
This creates further separation and possibly increases the lying in the future.

Option 2:
My kid lies to me.
I accept that my kid lied to me.
I don't make it mean any more than he lied.
I feel calm.
I tell him he is grounded and can't play videos for a week.
I am at peace.
He sees the action and the consequence and not my anger.
It is about him and his action/consequence—not about me.

Does that help?
I am happy to talk through this more.

Example four:

CLIENT: *Hi Brooke,*

I just listened to Self Coaching 101—thanks so much for making it available. I do have a question:

In the example of someone saying "I hate my job," you said there are two options —change the job or change the thought. Although I suspect changing the thought might always be appropriate in some way, aren't there are also times when changing the circumstance is indicated? How does one know when to do which?

Thanks!

BROOKE: Hi.

Great question. Always work the thoughts first. When you clean up your thoughts, you may find that you want to change you job—but you aren't deluding yourself into believing that your feelings come from your job or any other external source.

It is not that you change your job and then feel better, as it may seem. What happens is you change your job, your thoughts change and then you feel better. So you attribute feeling better to the job. This is a mistake. By understanding that your thoughts determine your feelings, you don't have to change your job to feel better. But you can change your job if you want a different job.

Make sense?

Brooke

CLIENT: *Yes, it does make sense, to clean up thoughts first. Among other things, it assures that I'm not responding from a sense of desperation ;-).*

Thanks for the answer.

Example five:

CLIENT: *Hi Brooke!*

Greetings from a college student in Hawaii. I just finished your book and have to say it is the BEST weight loss book I've read...and I've read A LOT of 'em. Your approach to it is exactly what I think so many of us need, but it is often overlooked because many of us think it is a "willpower" issue.

Anyway, I listened to yourself coaching class and had a question. How do we change a thought to something more positive if we aren't sure if it's true? Or if we are proven wrong?

For example, I'm having problems changing my thoughts about my ex-boyfriend. Although I don't WANT to be together with him, I still FEEL sad that he isn't trying to contact me. My thoughts are: This is not bothering him at all and he is over me. My feelings are: Hurt and unwanted. Actions: I don't contact him, either.

So my question is, how do I change that thought so I can truly believe it, if it's not true?

Thank you so much

BROOKE: Hi-

This is a great question to demonstrate finding the exact thought that is causing you pain. The thought I see here that is painful is this:

> My ex-boyfriend has not contacted me. (This is a circumstance)
> I am unwanted. (This is the painful thought)
> Hurt (This is the feeling)
> You don't contact him (action)
> You don't speak with him (result)—which helps you prove your original thought.

So all the work needs to be done on the thought "I am unwanted." This is the thought that needs work. Can you find a better feeling thought that is truer?

> I know lots of people who want to contact me.
> I want to contact me.
> I want me.
> If my ex-boyfriend contacted me, it wouldn't mean that I was want-worthy. His contacting me would tell me

more about HIS thoughts leading to his action of calling me and less about my worth. I am not contacting him and I don't want to be with him—but that doesn't mean he is unwanted.

CHAPTER 8

My Real Life

MODEL EXAMPLES

Here is some of my work using the self coaching model. The bold lines are where I started. This is actual work I did this past week:

Example of a painful thought I had this week.

Circumstance: Email from colleague requesting urgent action
Thought: **She has no right to be so demanding**
Feeling: Frustrated and disrespected
Action: Call my friend to complain
Result: Another negative thought: She doesn't appreciate how much I have to do.

New Thought: **She must need this for something important**
Feeling: Helpful
Action: Get it to her in a hurry
Result: Help my colleague and feel great about it

Example of a feeling I want to have this week

Circumstance: Going out of town with my good friend
Thought: She is a cherished treasure in my life
Feeling: **Connected and loving**
Action: Tell her how much she means to me. Pay attention to what I love about her.
Result: A deepened friendship with great conversations

Using the model for something I really want to have (result)

(I wrote the result in the model first and then filled in the rest of the model.)

Circumstance: School is starting next week
Thought: I provide a peaceful, loving and efficient home environment
Feeling: Competent, peaceful, loving
Action: Plan meals, schedule work while kids are at school, plan with kids' activities and preparation for the next day the night before
Result: **A weekly routine in place for kids once school starts**

Using the model for something I really want to believe

Circumstance:
Thought: **I will make more money with less effort this year**
Feeling: Excited, free, abundant
Action: Work smarter, work less and create more passive income products
Result: More income with less time spent working.

Using the model to motivate action

Desired Action: Writing

Circumstance: N/A
Thought: This book is almost done and will help people
Feeling: Excited
Action: **Writing**
Result: I wrote for five hours this week

Notes:

Conclusion

Your mind is a tool to use as you wish. Your mind does not have to be the one running the show; the part of you that watches your mind is a much better master and is aligned with your true intentions for this life. We may not understand our exact purpose for being alive, but we do know that feeling good makes the journey better.

As you use the self coaching model, you will learn how to think deliberately. You are not just learning how to dissolve a painful thought, but also how to create a new one that feels better and leads to different results. As you practice this, what you are really doing is practicing how to think. Practice your thinking. Lead your mind. You may have never heard this before. You may have never thought of thinking as something you can get good at, but it is.

The more your practice, the better you will get at deliberately thinking good feeling thoughts. As you feel better, you will take better action and get better results.

I had a client once tell me that she thought I was faking being so happy. This made me laugh out loud. I am not faking being happy—I don't have to. I am genuinely happy. I do work at it by managing my thoughts and consciously deciding what I choose to think so I can create a cycle of joy in my life. It has been a magical journey for me. I will never be able to go back to feeling out of control of my life or my joy.

I know that I am always just one thought away from relief. Some days it feels appropriate to be experiencing sadness or grief, and on those days I acknowledge my feelings and feel them deeply and fully. I know the thoughts causing them, and still I want to experience each and every feeling. This is very different than the suffering that comes from not knowing what is causing my feeling and trying to fight against myself. It feels clean and true and whole. When I live my life like this, the negative feeling states don't last very long and for the duration of their vibration in my body I notice that they aren't as painful as they used to be.

But on most days I am now filled with a deep sense of joy and peace. I laugh really hard quite often and smile at my luck every chance I get. It is my hope that this model will help you start your journey towards this type of joy for yourself. I have learned so much from my teachers and if I can help anyone else by sharing what I know, I am even more blessed than I imagined.

So find any place in your life that you don't believe is perfect, and plug that thought into the model. Do it again and again until one day you can't remember the last time you were filled with anxiety.

You are one thought away from the feeling you want.

Get it.

Appendix Worksheets

All of these worksheets are available on pdf through my website *www.brookcastillo.com*. Alternatively you can rip these worksheets out of this book and photocopy them to use often—whenever you have a thought that causes you discomfort.

WHEN THE PROBLEM SEEMS TO BE A CIRCUMSTANCE

What is the circumstance? ______________________________

____

____

What thought does the circumstance trigger? ______________________________

____

____

____

What do you feel when you think this thought? ______________________________

____

____

____

How do you act when you feel this way? ______________________________

____

____

____

What is the result of this action? ______________________________

____

____

____

How does the result prove the original thought? ______________________________

____

____

____

What is a better feeling thought to choose concerning this circumstance? ______________________________

____

____

Use the questions above to fill in the unintentional thought patterns.

UNINTENTIONAL THOUGHT PATTERN

CIRCUMSTANCE: ______________________________

____

____

THOUGHT: ______________________________

____

____

FEELING: ______________________________

____

____

ACTION: ______________________________

____

____

RESULT: ______________________________

____

____

INTENTIONAL THOUGHT PATTERN

CIRCUMSTANCE: ______________________________

____

____

NEW THOUGHT: ______________________________

____

____

FEELING: ______________________________

____

____

ACTION: ______________________________

____

____

RESULT: ______________________________

____

____

THOUGHT PROBLEM WORKSHEET

What is the negative **thought** you keep thinking? ____________________

____

____

____

What **feeling** does this thought cause you? ____________________

____

____

____

How do you **behave** when you feel this way? ____________________

____

____

____

What is the **result** of this action? ____________________

____

____

____

____

How does the result prove the original thought? ____________________

____

____

____

____

What is a better **feeling** thought to think that is believable to you? ____

____

____

____

Use the questions above to fill in the unintentional thought patterns.

UNINTENTIONAL THOUGHT PATTERN

CIRCUMSTANCE: ____________________

____

____

THOUGHT: ____________________

____

____

FEELING: ____________________

____

____

ACTION: ____________________

____

____

RESULT: ____________________

____

____

INTENTIONAL THOUGHT PATTERN

CIRCUMSTANCE: ____________________

____

____

NEW THOUGHT: ____________________

____

____

FEELING: ____________________

____

____

ACTION: ____________________

____

____

RESULT: ____________________

____

____

FEELING PROBLEM WORKSHEET

What is the negative feeling? ______________________________

____

What is the thought causing this feeling? ____________________

____

____

How do you act/react when you feel this way? _________________

____

____

What are the results of this action? _________________________

____

____

How does this result prove the original thought? _____________

____

____

What would you like to be feeling? ___________________________

____

____

What thought could you think/believe that would cause this feeling?

____

____

Use the questions above to fill in the unintentional thought patterns.

UNINTENTIONAL THOUGHT PATTERN

CIRCUMSTANCE: ______________________________

____

____

THOUGHT: ______________________________

____

____

FEELING: ______________________________

____

____

ACTION: ______________________________

____

____

RESULT: ______________________________

____

____

INTENTIONAL THOUGHT PATTERN

CIRCUMSTANCE: ______________________________

____

____

NEW THOUGHT: ______________________________

____

____

FEELING: ______________________________

____

____

ACTION: ______________________________

____

____

RESULT: ______________________________

____

____

ACTION PROBLEM WORKSHEET

What is the behavior you want to change? ____________________

____

____

____

What feelings do you experience prior to and during this behavior? __

____

____

____

____

What thoughts lead to this feeling and this behavior? (Answer anything here but "I don't know." Guess if you aren't sure.)__________

____

____

What result do you get when you act this way?________________

____

____

How does this result prove the original thought that leads to this behavior? ____________________________________

____

What feelings might negate this behavior? ___________________

____

____

What thought would you need to think to feel this way? ___________

____

____

Use the questions above to fill in the unintentional thought patterns.

UNINTENTIONAL THOUGHT PATTERN

CIRCUMSTANCE: ____________________

THOUGHT: ____________________

FEELING: ____________________

ACTION: ____________________

RESULT: ____________________

INTENTIONAL THOUGHT PATTERN

CIRCUMSTANCE: ____________________

NEW THOUGHT: ____________________

FEELING: ____________________

ACTION: ____________________

RESULT: ____________________

RESULT PROBLEM WORKSHEET

What is a negative result you currently have in your life? __________

____

____

What action leads to this result? ______________________________

____

____

What feelings cause this action? ______________________________

____

____

What thoughts cause this feeling? _____________________________

____

____

What is the opposite of this current thought? ____________________

____

____

What result would the opposite thought create? __________________

____

____

What is the result you want to have? __________________________

____

____

What is the thought you can think and believe to achieve this result?

____

____

____

Use the questions above to fill in the unintentional thought patterns.

UNINTENTIONAL THOUGHT PATTERN

CIRCUMSTANCE: ______________________________

____

____

THOUGHT: ______________________________

____

____

FEELING: ______________________________

____

____

ACTION: ______________________________

____

____

RESULT: ______________________________

____

____

INTENTIONAL THOUGHT PATTERN

CIRCUMSTANCE: ______________________________

____

____

NEW THOUGHT: ______________________________

____

____

FEELING: ______________________________

____

____

ACTION: ______________________________

____

____

RESULT: ______________________________

____

____

BONUS WORKSHEET

This is a practice I recently started and wanted to share with you. In addition to the work of writing down everything you want in you life, also try this: Write a list of thoughts you want to believe.

Here are some of mine, to give you an idea of what I mean:

Everything I need is within me now.
It's already done.
It's way better than I can even imagine.
Everything happens in perfect timing.
I create money with my thoughts.
Everything in my life happens for me.
I love deeply and those I love know it.
I don't ever need to try.
When aligned in my thinking, what I want is seemingly effortless.
Nothing has ever gone wrong.
I have more than I want to spend.
I am in perfect health.
This is my perfect body to live my life.
Everyone in my life is perfect and right on time.
I can feel the unlimited abundance within me.
My abundance helps the abundance of thousands of people.
The only difference between me and some others is that I know how lucky we are.
What they do is about them and what I do is about me.
They are truly doing the best they can and when they know better they will do better.
The Universe has got it covered. I can relax.

Now it's your turn:

1. ____

2. ____

3. ____

4. ____

5. ____

6. ____

7. ____

8. ____

9. ____

10. ____

If you want more information on what I am up to or on upcoming workshops and retreats, please check out www.brookecastillo.com and subscribe to my mailing list or blog. I will never spam you and will only send emails when I have something new to tell you. I love hearing from you (especially if you have nice things to say). You can email me directly at brooke@coach4weight.com.

May all your thoughts bring you freedom....

–Brooke